Are You

# THE EVIL
# NEXUS

## WARREN HENDERSON

All Scripture quotations are from the New King James Version of the Bible, unless otherwise noted. Copyright © 1982 by Thomas Nelson, Inc. Nashville, TN

*The Evil Nexus – Are You Aiding the Enemy?*
By Warren Henderson
Copyright © 2014

Cover Design: Ben Bredaweg
Editing/Proofreading: Mike Attwood,
    David Lindstrom, Dan Macy, and
    Kathleen Henderson

Published by Warren A. Henderson
3769 Indiana Road
Pomona, KS 66076

Perfect Bound ISBN 978-1-939770-26-4
eBook ISBN 978-1-939770-27-1

ORDERING INFORMATION:
Gospel Folio Press
Phone 1-905-835-9166
E-mail: order@gospelfolio.com
**Also available in many online retail stores**

Printed in the United States

# Other Books by the Author

Afterlife – What Will It Be Like?

Answer the Call – Finding Life's Purpose

Behold the Saviour

Be Angry and Sin Not

Conquest and the Life of Rest – A Devotional Study of Joshua

Exploring the Pauline Epistles

Forsaken, Forgotten, and Forgiven – A Devotional Study of Jeremiah

Glories Seen & Unseen

Hallowed Be Thy Name – Revering Christ in a Casual World

Hiding God – The Ambition of World Religion

In Search of God – A Quest for Truth

Knowing the All-Knowing

Managing Anger God's Way

Mind Frames – Where Life's Battle Is Won or Lost

Out of Egypt – A Devotional Study of Exodus

Overcoming Your Bully

Passing the Torch – Mentoring the Next Generation

Revive Us Again – A Devotional Study of Ezra and Nehemiah

Seeds of Destiny – A Devotional Study of Genesis

The Bible: Myth or Divine Truth?

The Fruitful Bough – Affirming Biblical Manhood

The Fruitful Vine – Celebrating Biblical Womanhood

The Hope of Glory – A Preview of Things to Come

The Olive Plants – Raising Spiritual Children

Your Home the Birthing Place of Heaven

# Table of Contents

The Evil Nexus ................................ 3

The Ongoing Unseen Confict ............... 9

#1 Disobedience ............................ 21

#2 False Accusations ...................... 33

#3 Slander .................................. 47

#4 Strife and Division .................... 57

#5 Blasphemy ............................... 65

#6 Deception and Lying ................... 81

#7 Gossip ................................... 89

The Real Enemy of the Real Battle .... 95

Endnotes .................................... 99

# Preface

If you are unfamiliar with the word *Nexus*, it speaks of a connection or a network which links two or more things together. *The Evil Nexus* investigates seven ways that Christians can, often unwittingly, be unnaturally linked with the devil to accomplish his wicked agenda.

Peter warned the Christians of his day to be alert because the enemy of their souls, the devil, was constantly prowling about to devour them: *"Be sober, be vigilant; because your adversary the devil walks about like a roaring lion, seeking whom he may devour"* (1 Pet. 5:8-9). Paul sharply rebuked believers in Galatia for their destructive conduct towards each other: *"But if you bite and devour one another, beware lest you be consumed by one another!"* (Gal. 5:15). The Greek word *katesthio*, translated as "devour" in both verses, means "to eat down." Stirred up in their flesh, the Galatians were imitating the devil's behavior; they were, to all practical purposes, cannibalizing each other! Regrettably, this onslaught among Christians continues to this day. The Christian community is the only army on earth which regularly permits the assault and slaughter of its own soldiers, resolutely ignores their wounded, and abandons their MIAs (those Missing in Action).

Dear believer, is it possible that you are actively, perhaps ignorantly, harming the body of Christ through devil-like behavior? Instead of being an ambassador of the Lord Jesus Christ on earth, could you be the puppet of Satan, wreaking havoc in the Church? Is it possible that your envy, critical spirit, and pride have blinded you to the fact that you have become a meat cleaver in the devil's hand to hack down the bride of Christ? Is the devil using you as bullhorn to incite his evil agenda in others? Peer down, look closely: is the splattered blood of your

# The Evil Nexus

brethren soiling your self-righteous attire? Oh God, deliver us from the pagan sacrilege of offering such blood sacrifices to the god of this age!

The author hardly knows a diligent servant of the Lord that has not gone through deep water. Many full-time workers have been falsely accused of wrong-doing, others slandered without regard to evidence or the due process of Scripture. Some have fallen into sin and have been devoured by the elite zealot wolfpack instead of being restored to productivity in a spirit of gentleness (Gal. 6:1). Such destructive "holy zeal" is causing the Lord's people to withdraw from service, and from each other. Some are now fearful to storm the gates of hell with the gospel, lest they be again shot in the back by "friendly fire."

Beloved of the Lord, this carnage must stop! The Lord said, *"every city or house divided against itself will not stand"* (Matt. 12:25). This would include the House of God, the Church. How can the Church, which is to represent Christ to a world that desperately needs to see Him, stand when believers are devouring each other? Such behavior honors Satan, not the Lord Jesus. May God help each one reading this book to consider his or her doings and for the glory of God initiate appropriate corrective action – no believer should be in cahoots with the devil! To aid the enemy is to oppose Christ!

# The Evil Nexus

Much of the Bible's teaching of who Satan is and what business he is really about has been obscured by world religion, fictional writings, and the media's fanciful productions. In many circles the devil is no more than an amusing comic book character – a make-believe creature attired in a one-piece red suit, having two daunting horns, a lengthy tail, and an ominous pitchfork. Viewing childhood cartoons and watching movies which wrongly depict him has resulted in many having a distorted view of who Satan actually is.

Many think he is merely a fictitious character, who like Santa Claus was created for childhood amusement or was developed by pious zealots to scare people into religious exploits. This, of course, is all part of Satan's masterful plan to further lull humanity, especially the Church, into a passive and despondent state, which is unconcerned about spiritual and eternal matters (2 Cor. 4:4). A more direct assault or direct revelation of his presence would awaken humanity to the real war that is raging in realms beyond their natural comprehension.

Regarding the Church, Satan has a well-furnished toolbox of clever tactics to keep Christians preoccupied so that they have little time, resources, or energy to further the Kingdom of God: materialism, fashion, sports, entertainment, amusements, sensuality, and education. It is not that any of these things are evil in themselves, but rather their intoxicating, habit-forming, lust motivating influence on Christians is the issue. When believers are tricked into trading the eternal for the temporal and first-love devotion for carnal thrills, Satan has successfully furthered his agenda. Unfortunately, the devil's deceptive propaganda has also muddled the Church's understanding of who their enemy

## The Evil Nexus

really is and the business he is about. In April of 2009, The Barna Group released a nationwide survey of 1,871 individuals who identified themselves as Christians.

All 1,871 self-described Christians were asked about their perception of God. In total, three-quarters (78%) said he is the "all-powerful, all-knowing Creator of the universe who rules the world today." ... Four out of ten Christians (40%) strongly agreed that Satan "is not a living being but is a symbol of evil." An additional two out of ten Christians (19%) said they "agree somewhat" with that perspective. A minority of Christians indicated that they believe Satan is real by disagreeing with the statement: one-quarter (26%) disagreed strongly and about one-tenth (9%) disagreed somewhat. The remaining 8% were not sure what they believe about the existence of Satan.[1]

In a poll of the general American populous, the Barna Group also found that just twenty-seven percent of American adults were convinced that Satan was a real force. Only forty percent of individuals who identify themselves as "born again" (i.e. evangelicals) were found to believe that perspective.[2] In summary, the greater majority of the professing Church does not believe that Satan is a real person or is even an ungodly influence which has a wicked agenda against them. Secondly, many who do believe that Satan exists cling to an unbiblical understanding of who he actually is. No wonder the western Church, generally speaking, is powerless; most identifying with Christ have no idea that they are in an intense spiritual battle. Yet, a tremendous war rages beyond their comfortable materialistic world. Bible commentator Donald Barnhouse explains:

> One of Satan's characteristic stratagems is to give those who believe that he does exist an entirely wrong concept of what his true nature and character really are. In the Middle Ages, when there were no radios, no magazines, no newspapers, no movies, no telephones, and none of our modern means of

# The Evil Nexus

passing the time, the people were frequently amused by the miracle plays. These were a sort of religious pageant in which religious stories were acted out on the stage. The audience learned to look for one character on the stage who was always dressed in red, wore horns on his head, and a tail dangling out behind him. His hoofs were cloven, and he had a pitchfork in his hand. The onlookers were quite thrilled when they saw this figure sneaking up on the hero or the heroine. The idea arose that Satan could be called the "old Nick," or "his satanic majesty," and that he was a slightly comic character.[3]

Is it possible for blood-bought sinners saved by grace to be in cahoots with the devil? Can Christians unknowingly do the devil's work and thus bestow honor to him? The answer to both of these questions, as we will see in the following chapters, is unequivocally "Yes." When we engage in such behavior, we literally become "little devils"; we have put ourselves in subjection to the one who hates God and is committed to disdaining His name. How it must wound the heart of God when His own children behave as they previously did before regeneration, that is, as children of the devil (Eph. 1:2-3; 1 Jn. 3:10).

In the following chapters we will explore seven prominent ways in which the children of God can align themselves with the devil and actually represent his interests through their ungodly behavior. Such conduct not only affects individual believers, but also has a devastating effect on the Church as a whole and disgraces its Head – the Lord Jesus Christ.

Furthermore, it is possible to respond to someone else who is engaging in one of these behaviors and thus be influenced to waste time on non-eternal matters and unknowingly become a participant in the devil's program. If the devil cannot solicit Christians to sin, he may use someone else to pull them into worthless activities. If we abandon the "best" for the "good," or the "good" for the "permissible" we have erred. For example, if we are lured from our God-sanctioned ministry to defend ourselves against false accusations, Satan gains a victory because the work of God is neglected and the disunity that results is a

## The Evil Nexus

poor presentation of God's holy character. The lost masses of humanity need to see Christ in His people, not more of what they are accustomed to enduring.

May each believer consider their conduct and be able to look beyond the visible realm to the real battle that is raging in heavenly places. In the balances of eternity, there is much more at stake presently than our creature comforts, our personal rights, our family reputations, or being proven innocent of wrongdoing. It is only through obedience, submission to authority, and brokenness that we experience reviving power and God's protection:

*For thus says the High and Lofty one who inhabits eternity, whose name is Holy: "I dwell in the high and holy place, with him who has a contrite and humble spirit, to revive the spirit of the humble, and to revive the heart of the contrite ones"* (Isa. 57:15).

*He who dwells in the secret place of the Most High shall abide under the shadow of the Almighty* (Ps. 91:1).

Hence, every satanic device employed against the believer affords him or her an opportunity to draw near to God and experience the wonder of His fellowship and the power of His deliverance. These wonderful blessings are lost to some degree when we withdraw from the intimate secret place of the Most High to defend ourselves, or worse, resort to the same debased behavior of our oppressors. Carnality opposed in the flesh can only have one outcome – more carnality: *"the wrath of man does not produce the righteousness of God"* (Jas. 1:20).

The Jews returning to Jerusalem after seventy years of Babylonian exile to rebuild the temple realized that this method of warfare would end in disaster. They had no army, no weapons, and were greatly outnumbered by their enemies, who had no desire to see a temple honoring Jehovah erected. Instead of strategizing a defense against their adversaries, the Jews committed themselves to understanding and submitting to what God

## The Evil Nexus

expected of them as His covenant people. For instance, they learned that Jehovah's Law required them to offer Him morning and evening sacrifices (Ex. 29:38-46; Ezra 3:3-6). They did not have a temple, but the Jews comprehended that it was through the daily offerings that God had been able to dwell in the midst of His people previously. Even if there was neither temple nor mercy-seat for God to dwell above and between the cherubim, the efficacy of the burnt offerings still remained as long the Jews continued to offer by faith as the Law demanded.

As the Jews were surrounded by opposition in their own homeland, it took great courage to raise an altar and begin sacrificing on it after fifty years. Militarily speaking, they were unarmed and outnumbered; their only defense was Jehovah. It is during this time frame (the third year of King Cyrus) that Daniel, still in Babylon, is made aware of the intense angelic battle raging beyond what is seen, the outcome of which would determine the affairs of men (Dan. 10). Indeed, an intense battle for the control of Jerusalem, the place where Jehovah had chosen to place His name, commenced when the Jews began offering sacrifices to Him again. Satan understood that once God's people were again obedient to His revealed will, they would be unbeatable. Surely God's people were far safer then, than when Jerusalem in her glory was surrounded by her fortified walls.

Likewise today, when God's people become desperate for Him, the spiritual warfare associated with their obedience becomes intense. Christians, therefore, would be wise to remain in the intimate presence of the Almighty by committing themselves to knowing and obeying God's Word, rather than deserting that privileged place of communion and blessing to hold hands with the devil (1 Cor. 10:20-21). There is a personal cost associated with obedience, but they that sow tears in God's presence shall ultimately reap joy (Ps. 126:5). Regrettably, many Christians are being ignorantly duped into a satanic agenda which hinders the work of God, damages the Church, and imparts disdain on the name of the Lord Jesus Christ.

## The Evil Nexus

Before reviewing these devilish tactics, it behooves us first to have a biblical view of the spiritual realm and the confrontation occurring there. As this domain is beyond our senses and natural reasoning, a panoramic view of Scripture is necessary to obtain an accurate understanding of what activities are ongoing there, and what bearing these have on humanity.

# The Ongoing Unseen Conflict

The Bible supplies many insights to the heavenly abode of God. John received a vision of heaven and describes for us what he saw in Revelation 4 and 5. Though each member of the trinity is omnipresent, a visual manifestation of their glory is witnessed for the purpose of focusing all worship in heaven on its appropriate center – God the Father, God the Son, and God the Spirit. The spectacular outshining glory of the Father is described (Rev. 4:3, 5:1). The Lord Jesus Christ who is seated at the right-hand of the Father upon His Father's throne is receiving the worship and praise of the hosts of heaven (Heb. 1:3; Rev. 3:21, 5:6-14). The Spirit of God (i.e. the Holy Spirit) is pictured before the throne as seven brilliant flames of fire (Rev. 4:5). Thus, the adoration of all holy spiritual beings and redeemed mankind in God's heavenly abode is directed towards the Godhead.

The heavenly spectacles and glorious sights that John witnessed in his visions were overwhelming to his senses at times. On one occasion, a confused John fell at his feet to worship one of the Lord's glorified servants who was speaking with him. He was immediately reproved:

> *And I fell at his feet to worship him. But he said to me, "See that you do not do that! I am your fellow servant, and of your brethren who have the testimony of Jesus.* **Worship God!** *For the testimony of Jesus is the spirit of prophecy"* (Rev. 19:10).

It is God alone that is to be worshipped, not heavenly beings or redeemed men. The Creator is to be honored by all His creatures (Rev. 5:13) and in fact all creation is to praise God (Ps. 98:8; Isa. 55:12).

# The Evil Nexus

## The Heavenly Ministries of Spiritual Beings

John provides a panoramic description of God's heavenly throne room. He speaks of the four living creatures, which each have one of four faces and six wings. These spiritual beings fly above the throne of God to continually declare God's holiness: *"Holy, holy, holy, Lord God Almighty, who was, and is, and is to come"* (Rev. 4:8). Besides this reference to the four living creatures, the Bible informs us that there are classes of spiritual beings that exist in heaven. In addition to Michael the archangel (Jude 9), there are cherubim (Gen. 3:24; Ezek. 1:5-14, 10:7), seraphim (Isa. 6:1-7), and a host of innumerable angels (Rev. 5:11).

Furthermore, Scripture describes to us the specific roles of these spiritual beings and how they appear before God's throne in heaven. For example, the angel Gabriel announced the births of both the Lord Jesus and John the baptizer. The four living creatures and seraphim have the occupation of flying about God's throne and praising His name, while cherubim are protectors of God's glory (i.e. they keep what is defiled from entering too close to and being consumed by divine holiness). Holy angels have various functions, such as ministering to God, praising Him, and being His messengers (Ps. 103:19-22); they also guard children to some degree from Satanic attack (Matt. 18:10). All things recorded in Scripture have purpose, so why did God go to such effort to afford us these details? What is it that He wants us to learn?

It is my opinion that the Father is calling our attention to His Son through the appearance of these extraordinary heavenly creatures. That is, their intrinsic glories are concealed by their wings to ensure our attention remains focused on the Lamb of God, the Lord Jesus Christ. For example, the Seraphim have six wings, but only use two for flying (Isa. 6). The Cherubim were given four wings, but they also use only two for flying (Ezek. 1). God intended them to use their remaining wings to cover their own intrinsic glories while in His presence, thus assuring that only He would be adored and worshipped in heaven. The

## The Ongoing Unseen Conflict

Church is to emulate this same practice when in God's presence, that is, salute God's creation order by covering competing glories, so that God's glory is seen (1 Cor. 11:2-16). Normally, these spiritual beings gladly cover themselves in God's presence, but there was a time when Lucifer, a special covering cherub, refused to cover himself and was lifted up in pride against God (Ezek. 28:13-16). He led a rebellion in heaven and likely took a third of the angels with him when he was cast out of God's presence (Isa. 14:12-15; Rev. 12:3-4, 9). These fallen angels have various biblical distinctions and evil agencies: demons, spirits of divination, foul spirits, unclean spirits, and familiar spirits.

The scriptural accounts of the cherubim in Ezekiel 1 and 10, of the seraphim in Isaiah 6, and of the four living creatures in Revelation 4 all disclose that these beings have four kinds of faces. Apparently, the cherubim each have all four, that is, the face of a lion, the face of an ox, the face of a man, and the face of an eagle. The faces of these beings reflect the same glories of the Lord Jesus that are presented in the main themes of each Gospel. The *lion* is the king of the beasts, which reflects Matthew's perspective of Christ as king. The *ox*, a beast of burden harnessed for the rigors of serving, pictures Mark's presentation of Jesus Christ, the servant. The face of the *man* clearly agrees with Luke's prevalent theme of the Lord's humanity. Lastly, the *eagle* flies high above all the other creatures – the divine essence of the Savior is in view here, as in the gospel of John. The many eyes of the cherubim describe Christ's omniscience and their bronze feet convey His divine authority to judge the wicked in flaming vengeance (Rev. 1:15). All that the Bible describes to us about heaven, whether in structures, furnishings, or angelic beings is for the purpose of calling our attention to the glory of God, especially witnessed in God's Son, who is the central message of the Bible (Rev. 19:10)!

# The Evil Nexus

## The Heavenly Ministries of Christ

While Christ's priestly work of providing propitiation for sinners is complete (Rom. 3:25; 1 Tim. 2:5), His continuing ministry in heaven as Priest is not. There are two main facets of this ongoing priestly ministry, namely, Christ as our *High Priest* and Christ as our *Advocate*. Speaking of the Lord Jesus, the writer of Hebrews declares:

> *Seeing then that we have a great High Priest who has passed through the heavens, Jesus the Son of God, let us hold fast our confession. For we do not have a High Priest who cannot sympathize with our weaknesses, but was in all points tempted as we are, yet without sin. Let us therefore come boldly to the throne of grace, that we may obtain mercy and find grace to help in time of need* (Heb. 4:14-16).

According to John, the Lord Jesus is also the believer's Advocate in heaven:

> *And if anyone sins, we have an Advocate with the Father, Jesus Christ the righteous* (1 Jn. 2:1-2).

## High Priest

As High Priest, Christ perfectly represents man to God: *"For every high priest taken from among men is appointed for men in things pertaining to God, that he may offer both gifts and sacrifices for sins"* (Heb. 5:1). A High Priest, then, stands between God and man, and must have a perfect connection with both in order to perform his duties properly. For this reason, the Aaronic priesthood and its offerings were inferior. Every priest after the order of Aaron was a sinner, and the blood of the bulls and goats that was presented in the temple on behalf of sinners could only atone for (cover) sin (i.e. the blood of animals could not cleanse a sinner's guilty conscience or provide propitiation for sins). Consequently, a new High Priest and a new Sacrifice were necessary: Christ was both (Heb. 7:27, 9:11-15, 24-26).

# The Ongoing Unseen Conflict

He was *"a merciful and faithful High Priest in things pertaining to God, to make propitiation for the sins of the people"* (Heb. 2:17). As a perfect Sacrifice, He not only exhibited divine moral perfection, but He was a man and, therefore, could legitimately substitute for humanity and be punished in our stead. Through one man's disobedience (Adam's), death engulfed humanity, but through one Man's obedience (Christ's), humanity received the opportunity for eternal life (Rom. 5:12-21).

He would be much more than a mere man and accomplish what no man could. As prophesied by Old Testament prophets, God would institute a New Covenant with His people that would give them eternal salvation, a new and clean heart, and allow the Holy Spirit to indwell them forever (Isa. 45:17-19; Jer. 31:31-40; Ezek. 34:25). Christ, as High Priest, sealed this covenant with the house of Judah and the house of Israel with His own blood (Luke 22:20; Heb. 8:8). As Paul explains in Ephesians 2 and 3, the Gentiles have been brought into the good of this New Covenant as a second benefactor. Consequently, our claim to the Lord Jesus as our High Priest is as strong as the claim of any redeemed Jew (Heb. 4:14). The Lord Jesus Christ is the Mediator of the New Covenant – He is our Great High Priest.

**Advocate**

Besides being our heavenly High Priest, Christ is also our legal representative or "Advocate" before the Father (1 Jn. 2:1). The English term "advocate" is only translated once from the Greek word *parakletos*, which is translated as "comforter" four times in John's gospel account in reference to the Holy Spirit. The role of advocate (or comforter) is to legally plead a case or to speak on the behalf of another in a court of law – a legal intercessor. Thayer's Greek definition describes the meaning as "Christ's pleading for pardon of our sins before the Father."[1] Concerning the Lord Jesus' continuing ministry of advocacy, S. Emery writes:

## The Evil Nexus

His valid ministry, therefore, on our behalf, is not on the basis of an effective, verbal and persuasive pleading before the Father, but on the basis of a perfect satisfaction for all our sins ever before the Father's face. He is our propitiation of undiminishing value. ... His very presence before the Father is the plea. Continuance in the family of God is never in question, but forgiveness of our sins, and cleansing from all unrighteousness, is experienced only when we make confession (1 Jn. 1:9).[2]

When does Christ plead our case? Is it when we acknowledge and confess our sins? 1 John 2:1 states that Christ is our advocate when we sin, not when we confess our sins, though we certainly should repent and confess our sins. The judgment of sin at Calvary and the empty tomb of Christ sufficiently answer any judicial claim the enemy may levy against a redeemed soul. Neither Satan nor the world has any claim on the Christian, for, positionally speaking, he or she has died and has been buried with Christ (Rom. 6:3-6). All our adversary's accusations against us are completely answered by our Advocate, Jesus Christ: His suffering and death were just payment for all of our offenses, and His resurrection, proof that God was satisfied with His redemptive work.

*And if anyone sins, we have an Advocate with the Father, Jesus Christ the righteous. And He Himself is the propitiation for our sins, and not for ours only but also for the whole world* (1 Jn. 2:1-2).

Positionally, all believers have been raised up with Christ and are presently seated with Him in heavenly places (Eph. 2:5-6). Christ's victory over the world is complete and we in Him are to continue delighting in and declaring that glorious fact day by day: *"These things I have spoken to you, that in Me you may have peace. In the world you will have tribulation; but be of good cheer, I have overcome the world"* (John 16:33). Each redeemed soul has the present opportunity to live out Christ's life by faith (Gal. 2:20); this is *victorious Christian living*! May each believer strive for this cause, until Christ concludes His priestly ministry by returning to the earth again to receive His Church, which will be the consummation of our salvation – glorification of the body (Phil. 3:21; Heb. 9:28).

## The Heavenly Activities of Satan

Why should the advocacy of the Lord Jesus Christ be a special comfort to every believer? Because Satan continually accuses believers before God's throne day and night (Rev. 12:10). When a believer sins, Satan abruptly calls God's attention to the despicable deed, but Christ is at the right hand of God the Father. He also acknowledges the unrighteous behavior of the believer but then states that the penalty for this lawless deed has already been paid by Himself at Calvary. In this way, all heavenly hosts, powers, and principalities witness that God is righteous and that He has accounted justly for every wrong the believer has done. James Gunn writes in his book *Christ the Fullness of the Godhead*:

> Christ is not a mere suppliant petitioner. He pleads for us on the grounds of justice, of righteousness, of obedience to the law, and endurance of its full penalty for us, on which He grounds His claim for our acquittal. The sense therefore is, "in that He is righteous."[3]

God hates sin, but because He judged Christ for human sin, He can extend the repentant sinner a full pardon and family status as His adopted child (Rom. 8:15). Though we never need to fear the judicial penalty of our sins being laid upon us, we will long to live in holiness before our Father so as to stay in fellowship with Him and to not provoke His chastening hand. Our souls have been liberated through the work of Christ to serve God out of love and not out of fear of judgment, for judgment is past and true love does not fear (1 Jn. 4:18).

# The Evil Nexus

Some may be shocked to learn that Satan, the epitome of evil, still has access to God's holy abode in heaven. It is the author's opinion that no evil could come into God's intimate presence without being consumed, and thus God's glory is veiled by clouds and darkness (Ps. 18:11, 97:2) to the one who is the "Father of Lies" (John 8:44). It is emphasized that Satan serves God despite his proud rebellious nature. Even through accusing the brethren, as we have already seen, the righteousness of God is substantiated.

Job chapter 1 records two conversations that God had with Satan in heaven. Both indicate that Satan, as a created being, remains under God's authority. God only permitted Satan to go so far in testing Job. The world is Satan's delegated domain, but he must function within the boundaries which God allows. This is why the world generally tolerates religion (i.e. save- or improve-yourself mentalities), but stands in opposition to Jesus Christ and His message (i.e. we are condemned without a Savior). This is why Christ is excluded from conversations, education, professional realms, etc., while it is permissible to speak about any of the world's religions. This is all Satan's doing; he is behind the scenes controlling the various systems of the world, and he despises Christ and those who take His name. Paul properly identifies Satan as *"the god of this age"* (2 Cor. 4:4) and *"the prince of the power of the air"* (Eph. 2:2). The Lord Jesus says on three different occasions that Satan is *"the prince of this world."*

There is no evidence in Scripture that Satan ever lies to God; his statements and accusations before the throne are accurate. He knows that he cannot deceive God, and that such behavior would invoke His wrath. This likely explains why God, after the fall of mankind, did not interrogate the serpent in Eden (Gen. 3). God already knew the truth and there was nothing to be gained by questioning the one already eternally condemned for his rebellion (Isa. 14:12-15; Matt. 25:41). However, when speaking with humanity, Satan lies, deceives, falsely accuses, and presents half-truths and rebellion-provoking questions

## The Ongoing Unseen Conflict

(John 8:44; 2 Cor. 4:4, 11:13-15). In fact, the first question in the Bible belongs to Satan: *"Has God indeed said, 'You shall not eat of every tree of the garden'?"* (Gen. 3:1). By casting doubt on God's word, Satan was able to first lead the woman and then Adam into sin, which resulted in immediate spiritual death – separation from God. Hence, the Lord declared that Satan was a murderer from the beginning (John 8:44) – he murdered humanity in the spiritual sense. In rebellion against God, Lucifer has brought humanity nothing but pain, misery, suffering, and death!

**Application**

Understanding the ongoing confrontation in heavenly realms should cause the child of God to keep "short accounts" with God. As soon as one is conscious of sin, the sin should be confessed. The great preacher, C. H. Spurgeon, was once walking across a busy and dangerous street with another Christian man. Spurgeon stopped in the middle of the street, bowed his head momentarily, then lifted it up again and proceeded to walk across the street without saying a word. The man reproved him for stopping, saying, "What were you doing back there? It looked like you were praying." Spurgeon replied, "Indeed I was. A cloud came between me and my Savior, and I wanted to remove it even before I got across the street."[4] God desires His children not to sin (1 Jn. 2:1). But when we do sin, *"If we confess our sins, He is faithful and just to forgive us our sins, and to cleanse us from all unrighteousness"* (1 Jn. 1:9). While the believer's relationship is eternally secured in divine grace, let every child of God stay in active fellowship with his or her Father by living holy and confessing sin the moment he or she stumbles.

Lucifer is likely the most powerful created being; not even Michael the archangel would venture out of creation order to rebuke Satan, but rather he wisely said, *"The Lord rebuke you"* (Jude 9). We are much less powerful than angels: How can we possibly confront the evil power and deception of Satan on our

## The Evil Nexus

own? Paul tells believers that we do not war against flesh and blood, but rather against spiritual wickedness in high places which are beyond the earthly scene:

> *Finally, my brethren, be strong in the Lord and in the power of His might. Put on the whole armor of God, that you may be able to stand against the wiles of the devil. For we do not wrestle against flesh and blood, but against principalities, against powers, against the rulers of the darkness of this age, against spiritual hosts of wickedness in the heavenly places* (Eph. 6:10-12).

Victory is only possible when believers venture into heavenly places on their knees to receive power and wisdom from Him who is above all principalities and powers. Christians can do nothing without Christ (John 15:5), but can accomplish all that is approved of God through Him (Phil. 4:12). To war against spiritual wickedness in heavenly places we must rely on a higher authority than the enemy's – thus, the paramount importance of Christ's priestly ministry.

### Summary

Christ completed His prophetic ministry during His first advent to the earth – He soundly defeated the devil at Calvary (John 12:31-32) and again at His resurrection (Eph. 1:19-21). *"For this purpose the Son of God was manifested, that He might destroy the works of the devil"* (1 Jn. 3:8). As the living Word, He was both God's Message and Messenger to humanity; only through Him can repentant sinners be saved and obtain power to live for God, instead of the devil (John 14:6).

> *Inasmuch then as the children have partaken of flesh and blood, He Himself likewise shared in the same, that through death He might destroy him who had the power of death, that is, the devil, and release those who through fear of death were all their lifetime subject to bondage* (Heb. 2:14-15).

# The Ongoing Unseen Conflict

As our eternal High Priest, Christ continues to intercede in heaven on our behalf on the basis of the New Covenant sealed with His own blood. In so doing, He accomplished what the Old Testament sacrifices and the Aaronic priesthood never could. Because the Lord Jesus is the believer's High Priest, each child of God is invited to boldly approach His throne of grace to obtain mercy and grace in time of need (Heb. 4:16). Christians on this side of glory are not sinless, but as they draw near to and are sustained by Christ they will sin less. It is in this secret place that the believer finds comfort in suffering righteously for Christ and help to refrain from sin and the wherewithal to live for God. Children of God are marked by righteous living (i.e. they do not practice sin; 1 Jn. 3:8-9) and by their love for their fellow brethren:

> *In this the children of God and the children of the devil are manifest: Whoever does not practice righteousness is not of God, nor is he who does not love his brother* (1 Jn. 3:10).

Satan continues to accuse believers who have sinned before God's throne, but Christ's advocacy declares that though God is offended by the believer's sin, the judicial penalty for his or her sin has been paid in full. Thus, the very accusations of the enemy against us became the framework to uphold the glory of God for all to see!

I hear the accuser roar, of ills that I have done;
I know them well, and thousands more, Jehovah finds none.
Though the restless foe accuses – Sins recounting like a flood
Every charge our God refuses; Christ has answered with His blood.

— Unknown

When believers lower themselves to engage in the dirt-throwing behavior which honors the devil, there can be no winners; all involved just become miserably filthy: He who throws dirt just loses ground! At such times, it is not love, but disdain

## The Evil Nexus

for the brethren and Christ Himself which is demonstrated. It would be profitable for us to remember that the way we treat the lowliest child of God shows our true appreciation and esteem for the Savior (Matt. 25:40).

Only by divine wisdom and the manifestation of God's power within us can believers have victory over such a wicked and formidable enemy as Satan. For this reason, may all believers consider their doings. Are we bestowing honor and glory to the name of the Lord Jesus Christ, or are we actually aiding Satan's rebellion against God and his evil agenda against humanity through devilish behavior? The believer's positional unity in Christ demands that he or she have no behavioral nexus with the devil.

# #1 Disobedience

Previously, the Christians at Colossae had been "children of disobedience" engaging in such things as fornication, uncleanness, greed, and idolatry, and thus were destined to suffer God's wrath (Col. 3:5-7). Before trusting Christ as Savior, they had been under the devil's authority and hence willfully indulged in the evil to which he approved. Satan is the father of disobedience because he invented and initiated rebellion (1 Jn. 2:16). However, those who agree with God about the matter of sin and exercise faith in the gospel message receive His grace and are born again into His family (John 1:12-13). As God's children, we must submit to His rule and His Word to obtain His blessing. Those who have been born again should cease to behave as they previously did as children of disobedience under Satan's authority.

God's first warning to His covenant people after their redemption and deliverance from Egypt exemplifies this necessity: obedience would be rewarded, but disobedience would be punished (Ex. 15:26). Every child of God in the Church Age has the same choice: *"Therefore be imitators of God as dear children"* (Eph. 5:1); *"As obedient children, not conforming yourselves to the former lusts, as in your ignorance"* (1 Pet. 1:14); *"For whom the Lord loves He chastens, and scourges every son whom He receives"* (Heb. 12:6). But the devil does not surrender his former children easily, that is, those born into sin and disobedience because of the failure of our first parents. A review of their temptation and fall will enhance our understanding as to how the devil might entice us to likewise disobey our heavenly Father.

# The Evil Nexus

## The First Rebellion

The Bible begins and ends with a peaceful garden paradise in which God communes with His special creation called "man." Our first parents were placed in Eden, but unfortunately succumbed to the temptation of the devil to disobey God's Word. As a result they instantly experienced spiritual death, that is, their spiritual communion with God was severed. Man had been bestowed authority over a perfect world, but God would not have a perfect world ruled by a corrupted authority, thus He cursed that portion of creation which pertained to man, namely the earth. Adam and Eve were abruptly evicted from their garden paradise to toil and suffer in a world now spoiled by human sin.

Through the Lord Jesus Christ, God continues to labor throughout the Bible to justly deal with the penalty of sin and the vast damage it has and continues to cause. The closing pages of the book of Revelation inform us that God will be completely successful in this matter and will restore redeemed man into His intimate presence of eternal bliss, described as *"the Paradise of God"* (Rev. 2:7).

There were two notable trees within the first garden mentioned in Scripture: the Tree of Life and the Tree of the Knowledge of Good and Evil, which for mankind was a Tree of Death. Apparently (based on the narrative in Genesis 3), as one exercised faith in the partaking of the Tree of Life, rather than the Tree of Death, immortality of the body was maintained. Both trees likely presented low-hanging branches laden with accessible fruit. There was nothing magical in the fruit, but grace was imputed through an operation of faith in God's Word to do what was right instead of what was unlawful.

In Eden, God enjoyed walking and conversing with Adam in the cool of the day (Gen. 3:8). This blessed communion was tragically broken on the day man ignored God's only restriction for continued life with God in Eden. On that regretful day man ate from the prohibited Tree of the Knowledge of Good and Evil. The cost of savoring one bite of the forbidden fruit was

## #1 Disobedience

immensely high, for our first parents traded a refreshing eternal existence with God for a sorrow-filled and brief earthly sojourn. The first rebel led an angelic revolt against God and now assisted man in his rebellion. Satan side-stepped Adam's authority and directed his assault on the unprotected woman. Fueled by his own jealousy of God and His glory, Satan beguiled her through a barrage of deceptive tactics. His goal was to stir up self-focus and diminish her perceived need for God in an attempt to cause her to rebel against His authority.

### Rebel Tactics

Although his evil operations used today are often more high-tech, his core strategies against mankind have not changed since the dreadful day sin intruded humanity. With these he has been successful in causing some to err from the faith or embrace some Christ-defaming doctrine. Paul writes, *"Lest Satan should get an advantage of us: for we are not ignorant of his devices"* (2 Cor. 2:11). The believer must be wise to Satan's deceit. A study of his offensive against the woman will aid in highlighting many of his evil strategies used today to solicit us to ignore and thus disobey God's Word.

First, mark the miracle – the serpent spoke. So crafty was Satan's communication to Eve that she thought nothing unusual about the serpent being able to form human speech. Didn't she know that she was talking to a serpent? Until now, only God had communicated to mankind through speech. Beware, dear believer, of clever words uttered by those following Satan. Children of the devil are pernicious to the children of God – one must always expect malicious behavior (John 15:18-19). A serpent is a serpent – don't be deceived by crafty speech or the conjuring of some unusual sign. Those looking for signs and wonders to substantiate their faith invariably fall in the trap of ignoring God's immutable Word. Paul acknowledged that same dark practice when he walked upon the earth:

# The Evil Nexus

*For such are false apostles, deceitful workers, transforming themselves into apostles of Christ. And no wonder! For Satan himself transforms himself into an angel of light. Therefore it is no great thing if his ministers also transform themselves into ministers of righteousness, whose end will be according to their works* (2 Cor. 11:13-15).

Second, note that Satan projected doubt on what God actually said: *"And he said to the woman, 'Has God indeed said, "You shall not eat of every tree of the garden"?'"* (Gen. 3:1). Until this point, Scripture accounts God's creative acts and statements of truth. The first question in Scripture belongs to Satan. It was a leading question, for its purpose was not to provoke rational thought but to instill doubt and invoke rebellion. The tactic worked on the woman, who quickly slid from the ground of faith into human reasoning. Satan's question to the woman has a flavor of unfairness: "Could God be good and limit you in such an unfair way?" "Surely a good God would not keep you from all that is good." "Are you sure that you recalled exactly what God said?"

A third satanic strategy is seen in the focusing upon the negative rather than the positive. Man was invited to eat from every tree in the garden, save one. Yet, the serpent beckoned mankind to focus upon the only one off limits. Satan enjoys sowing dissatisfaction. When embraced, dissatisfaction stirs up doubts concerning God's goodness and wisdom. Dear believer, the next time Satan tempts you not to be content, train your eye upon all the blessings in Christ and not what, in your own mind, you lack or deserve.

Eve's reply to the serpent demonstrates a diminished view of God in her thinking. F. W. Grant writes concerning the woman's reply to the serpent:

> But here God and the dragon had changed places. Thus she adds to the prohibition, as if to justify herself against One who has lost His sovereignty for her heart, "You shall not eat of it, *neither shall ye touch it*" –which He had not said. A

# #1 Disobedience

mere touch, as she expressed it to herself, was death; and why, then, had He put it before them only to prohibit it? What was it He was guarding from them with such jealous care? Must it not be indeed something that He valued highly? She first adds to the prohibition, then she weakens the penalty. Instead of "you shall surely die," it is for her only *"lest* [for fear] you die." There is no real certainty that death would be the result. Thus the question of God's love becomes a question of His truth also. I do not want on the throne a being I cannot trust; hence comes the tampering with His word. The heart deceives the head. If I do not want it to be true, I soon learn to question if it be so.[1]

Fourth, notice Satan added to what God had said; *"Then the serpent said to the woman, "You will not surely die"* (Gen 3:4). The addition of one three-letter word changed God's intended meaning completely. God said, *"for in the day that you eat of it you shall surely die"* (Gen. 2:17), but Satan said, *"you will **not** surely die."* Satan was referring to physical death while ignoring the subject of spiritual life with God completely. God warned of immediate spiritual death, though physical death would naturally come to those apart from God. Every cemetery is proof that God told the full truth and that Satan is a liar. John Darby once declared, "The devil is never more satanic than when he has a Bible in his hands." Be careful when the enemy is quoting Scripture; the whole truth will never be presented!

A fifth tactic employed was the breaking down of Scripture into small pieces to obscure the contextual meaning of what God said. The truth of God's Word is found in the whole of Scripture. Browsing over minute portions alone can result in doctrines that are inconsistent with the remainder of Scripture. It has been said that there are three rules in selling real estate – "location, location, location." Likewise, there are three rules to determining what Scripture is saying – "context, context, context." The Bible as a whole presents a specific truth about God's plan of redemption for mankind. No passage of Scripture should be interpreted to contradict this central theme of the Bible, as

# The Evil Nexus

summarized in John 3:16. There is also a specific subject that each book of the Bible is addressing, so the understanding of a passage within that book should be in the context of the main theme. Finally, specific portions of Scripture must be interpreted by the encompassing verses to ensure correct understanding. Satan cast doubt on what God said, changed what God said, and only referred to select portions of what God said when speaking to the woman. Beware of those reducing divine revelation into obscurity.

Lastly, the "sales pitch" Satan used on the woman is no different than the one he is using today through the "New Age" movement. It is a "repackaged old lie," and it has worked on man since the beginning. Satan told the woman that she could improve her position, that she was in control of her destiny, that she could gain knowledge and understanding and be like God. How man scrambles at the chance to become like God and to have His power and might. Yet, the best man can do is bow in humility, accept God's salvation, and become a child of God.

It is obvious that Satan communicates throughout the Bible, but his actual voice is recorded only three times. In Genesis 3, he spoke to undermine and cast doubt on the Word of God. In Job 1, Satan spoke to undermine and cause the child of God to doubt. Lastly, in Matthew 4 the devil spoke to undermine and cast doubt concerning the Son of God. The summary of Satan's recorded communication in the Bible – three verbal attempts to cast doubt on what is righteous. Let us be wise to his deceit; do not doubt God's Word, dear believer, but rather trust and obey, even when it does not seem sensible to do so.

> When we walk with the Lord in the light of His Word,
> What a glory He sheds on our way!
> While we do His good will, He abides with us still,
> And with all who will trust and obey.
> Trust and obey, for there's no other way
> To be happy in Jesus, but to trust and obey.
> 
> — John Sammis

# #1 Disobedience

## Summary

Knowing that it is God's Word and God's Spirit that direct the course of each believer's life should prompt us to stay attentive to both. Satan can do nothing against the Holy Spirit, but believers grieve Him through willful sin (Eph. 4:30). Our wrong attitudes and behavior quenches His powerful communion within us (1 Thess. 5:19); in this weakened state the believer is vulnerable to satanic delusion and acting in the flesh. As in Eden, Satan continues today to cast doubt on God's Word. He may mask the deception with a supernatural feat, or pose questions which cause us to reason against what God has said or to doubt His goodness to us. He may also use micro-analysis or a deviant translation of Scripture to undermine the meaning of its plain language.

The author has been told by those in cults, "You know, we are not that much different in our beliefs." This is a common trick of Satan; he uses the disguise of a charitable cause or religious movement in an attempt to create an unnatural union between God's people and his. Jehoshaphat fell prey to this tactic (2 Chron. 18), as did the Israelites in the wilderness (Ex. 12:38; Num. 11:4-6). There can be no God-pleasing communion between the children of God and the children of the devil. Even the supposed good deeds of the latter are unacceptable to God, because the motivation for such acts originates, in varying degrees, from the impurity of their intrinsic fallen nature (Titus 1:15-16).

Believers, however, are exhorted to live up to their new family identification as children of God and children of light (i.e., truth) and not behave as they once did as children of the devil and children of disobedience:

*And you He made alive, who were dead in trespasses and sins, in which you once walked according to the course of this world, according to the prince of the power of the air, the spirit who now works in the sons of disobedience, among whom also we all once conducted ourselves in the lusts of*

## The Evil Nexus

*our flesh, fulfilling the desires of the flesh and of the mind, and were by nature children of wrath, just as the others* (Eph. 2:1-3).

Most of us have seen a drum major or majorette lead a marching band down a spectator-lined street during a parade. In your mind's eye picture Satan as a drum major who is leading a group of disorderly zombies down a wide way. This mob of ruffians follows their leader wherever he goes and does his bidding with uncanny fervency. These walking corpses eat his food, behave like him, walk like him, listen to his music, and enjoy his entertainment. The members of this band proudly engage in lying, stealing, blasphemy, and all sorts of lascivious behavior as they march along. Bang! Pound! Bam! The drums of rebellion sound; the cadence both energizes and enrages their rebel ranks. Where is this unruly mob headed? Their leader knows, but most of those following him have no idea that they're on a one-way trip to the Lake of Fire, a place created by God to punish Satan and his fallen angels (Matt. 25:41).

The devil's main ambition is to lead as many of those who bear the image of God away from Him and the salvation He offers. As Satan knows his doom is sealed (Rev. 12:12, 20:10), he is determined to lead as many as possible into hell's eternal flames (Rev. 13:15, 19:20-21). This parade imagery pictures man's natural state in the world. Prior to knowing Jesus Christ as Savior, we were members of this band; we were *"children of the devil"* (1 Jn. 3:10), *"children of disobedience"* (Eph. 2:2), and *"children of wrath"* (Eph. 2:3). God can have no fellowship with these children, for their allegiance, though at times unwittingly rendered, is to His arch-enemy. Consequently, we were all born into this world, not merely separated from God, but as His enemy (Rom. 5:10).

Only by trusting Christ and being born again can one become a child of God and change his or her family lineage (John 3:3). Afterwards, there is no reason for a child of God to ever want to return to the rebel zombie band and march in time

# #1 Disobedience

with unregenerate rebels. Unfortunately, through willful disobedience this occurs all too often and how Satan enjoys seeing blood-bought saints treading upon the very blood of their Savior (Heb. 6:6).

## The Christian Response to Disobedience

Satan has eroded the Church's foundation of sound doctrine through dozens of inaccurate or watered-down versions of the Bible in recent years. Many people now believe that, because there are so many Bible translations that they say "disagree," no one can know what God's Word actually is. This assessment is incorrect. In fact, ninety percent of the ancient manuscripts from which the Old Testament is derived are without any variants. The authenticity of the New Testament is substantiated by: 5,600 plus copies of Greek Manuscripts, 10,000 plus copies of Latin Vulgate, and 9,300 plus copies of early versions in other languages. Besides this, some 86,000 New Testament quotations exist by the early church fathers, the summation of which can produce the entire New Testament less eleven verses.[2] The New Testament writings are scientifically proven to 99.5 percent authenticity to the original autographs. In short, there is no other ancient book on the planet with the authenticity of the Bible! For this reason, it behooves Christians to read and study a good "literal" translation of the Bible (e.g. NKJV, NAS, ESV, KJV, etc.) to ensure that we are not being deceived by one of Satan's attempts to dilute or replace the meaning of what God has communicated to us, especially about Himself.

The paramount reason to study Scripture is to personally know the One who is all-knowing. Knowledge that "puffs up" is not the goal, but rather awareness of God's greatness which prompts us to fall on our faces in wonder and awe before Him. The reason Paul prayed that the Colossian believers would be *"increasing in the knowledge of God"* is that he knew such knowledge would lead them into spiritual wisdom, strength, and fruitfulness (Col. 1:9-11). Whenever a believer's understanding of God slips, or his or her desire to know God more intimately

## The Evil Nexus

wanes, something is very wrong. Understanding who God is, and what He has done and will do, promotes our spiritual vitality. Most of our doubts, anxieties, and disobedience arise from a diminished view of God's true nature. We must learn of Him and know what He expects to rightly please Him – this requires us to be regularly in His Word.

When God is shut out and man no longer allows God's love and truth to be recognized in his life, *"the lust of the flesh, the lust of the eyes, and the pride of life"* then become the controlling influences in that person's life. This is what happened to Eve – she doubted God's love and truth. All three of these agencies are from the world (1 Jn. 2:16) and Satan stimulates each to work his will. "The lust of the flesh, the lust of the eyes, and the pride of life" describe giving over one's flesh, mind and will to secular reasoning and influences instead of resting upon divine truth. Temptations thus may be directed against the body, the soul, or the spirit or at all three at once, as was the case with Eve.

When Satan externally solicited Christ to sin in the wilderness (Matt. 4), he utilized these three avenues because they had worked so well on mankind previously. Satan solicited the Lord Jesus to sin by an appeal to His body to satisfy its appetite. Satan's second attempt to solicit the Lord to sin was through an appeal to human spiritual pride. If the Lord would have thrown Himself off the top of the temple and the angels did scramble to save Him, it would have been a demonstration to the world that He was approved of God and would bring worldwide recognition and spiritual preeminence. The last fiendish attempt was aimed at the soul level – an appeal was made to stir up covetous and emotional desires for fame and prestige that the authority over kingdoms would ensure. Yet, Satan failed to cause Christ to sin because the Lord Jesus did not have the fallen human element that would respond to these solicitations – for Christ is God in the flesh. He was not merely born innocent as was Adam, but absolutely holy (Luke 1:35). It was His nature to loathe sin; He could not respond to such ill appeals, but we can!

# #1 Disobedience

The aggressive assault on the bulwark of divine character was completely thwarted by the use of exact and complete quotations from God's Word. For the believer to practically apply the Bible in this manner means that he or she must be constantly reading God's Word, studying it, meditating on it, memorizing it, and obeying it. The children of God do not need new revelation to know what God expects of them; we have His complete Word already. Jim Elliot puts the matter this way: "Why do you need a voice when you have a verse." Accordingly, the Psalmist proclaims the life and death importance of reading, mediating, and obeying God's Word:

*With my whole heart I have sought You; Oh, let me not wander from Your commandments* (Ps. 119:10)!

*I will never forget Your precepts, for by them You have given me life* (Ps. 119:93).

*Your word is a lamp to my feet and a light to my path* (Ps. 119:105).

*Your word is very pure; therefore Your servant loves it* (Ps. 119:140).

Solomon clearly summarizes the futility of disobedience:

*He who despises the word will be destroyed, but he who fears the commandment will be rewarded* (Prov. 13:13).

*There is a way that seems right to a man, but its end is the way of death* (Prov. 16:25).

Let every child of God then follow the Lord's example when solicited by Satan and lift up the shield of faith and appropriate the instruction and promises of God's Word to deflect the incoming fiery darts of temptation. For our first parents the temptation came in the form of a single question! Be alert; the

## The Evil Nexus

devil won't send you a text message to inform you of his secret battle tactics.

## Meditation

Our early Church fathers understood the importance of studying and memorizing God's Word. Knowing and obeying Scripture ensured that they would live a life honoring to the Lord and would also heighten their awareness to the devil's attempts of leading them into disobedience:

> The early Church father, **Tertullian** devoted his days and nights to Bible reading, so much so that he learned much of it by heart, even its punctuations.
> **Theodosius the Younger** could repeat any part of the Scripture exactly, and discourse with the bishops at court as if he himself were a bishop.
> **Origen** never went to meals or to sleep without having some portions of the Scriptures read.
> **Eusebius** said that he heard of one, whose eyes were burned out under the Diocletian persecution, repeat from memory the Scriptures in a large assembly.[3]

The golden rule for understanding in spiritual matters is not intellect, but obedience.

— Oswald Chambers

# #2 False Accusations

While it is important for all believers to avoid falsely accusing others, Paul specifically instructs Titus to admonish older women to avoid this destructive behavior: *"The aged women likewise, that they be in behavior as becometh holiness, not false accusers, not given to much wine, teachers of good things"* (Titus 2:3; KJV). Though we are all guilty of falsely accusing others, perhaps Paul felt this particular gender-age group was more prone to this sin than others were. The Greek word *diabolos*, which is normally translated "devil" in the New Testament, is rendered "false accusers" in this verse. Paul also foretells that in the last days of the Church Age the sin of false accusation will be prevalent (2 Tim. 3:3; KJV).

Francis Frangipane in his booklet *Exposing the Accuser of the Brethren* rightly acknowledges the devastating chaos that Satan has inflicted on the Church through the sin of falsely accusing others:

> More churches have been destroyed by the accuser of the brethren and its faultfinding than by either immorality or misuse of church funds. So prevalent is this influence in our society that, among many, faultfinding has been elevated to the status of a "ministry"! ... In an attempt to hinder, if not altogether halt the next move of God, Satan has sent forth an army of fault-finding demons against the Church [this is supposition]. The purpose of this assault is to entice the Body of Christ away from the perfection of Jesus and onto the imperfection of one another.
>
> This enemy is assigned to attack relationships on all levels. It attacks families, churches and inter-church associations, seeking to bring irreparable schisms into our unity. Masquerading

## The Evil Nexus

as discernment, this spirit will slip into our opinions of other people, leaving us critical and judgmental. Consequently, we all need to evaluate our attitude toward others. If our thoughts are other than faith working through love, we need to be aware that we may be under spiritual attack.

When this spirit infiltrates an individual's mind, its accusations come with such venom and "authority" even those who "know better" are seduced and then silenced by its influence. We are indifferent to the fact Jesus is praying for His body to become one. Beguiled by this demon, we circulate his accusations through a church-body or city, stimulating suspicion and fear among the people. We allow devastation to wrack the targeted ministry while discouragement blankets and seeks to destroy the Lord's servant and his family.

With the same zeal that the critical seek to unearth sin, those who will conquer this enemy must zealously know God's heart and his calling for each church. Indeed, the Lord's word to us is that fleshly criticism must be replaced with prayer, and fault-finding with a covering love. Where there is error, we must go with a motive to restore. Where there are wrong doctrines, let us maintain a gentle spirit correcting those in opposition.[1]

Any true work of God will be opposed by the devil! If you are rightly laboring for the Lord in your calling, you will be criticized and accused of wrongdoing; it is part of the faith-building exercise which God permits to develop His people. He is not the source of the allegations, but masterfully uses the ill will of Satan and impulses of our proud flesh to accomplish a greater good on our behalf. James reminds us that there is a quality of patience that cannot be incorporated into our faith without experiencing God's deliverance through such painful trials:

> *My brethren, count it all joy when you fall into various trials, knowing that the testing of your faith produces patience. But*

## #2 False Accusations

*let patience have its perfect work, that you may be perfect and complete, lacking nothing* (Jas. 1:2-4).

In regard to Jewish history, perhaps no greater attempt to hinder God's work through false accusations occurred than after the Jews returned from Babylonian captivity to rebuild the temple and the city of Jerusalem. The priest Ezra notes that the enemy steadily confronted Jewish resolve from the time of King Cyrus to the reign of Artaxerxes, well over a century (Ezra 4:4-24). He specifically mentions three letters that were written to falsely accuse the Jews of wrongdoing. Although he merely references the first letter written in the days of King Ahasuerus (Ezra 4:6), he does provide the contents of the other two letters drafted during the reigns of Darius and Artaxerxes. The former was written by the enemy to stop the rebuilding of the temple in the sixth century BC and the latter to stop the rebuilding of Jerusalem in the fifth century BC. Examination of these letters reveals much about how the tactic of false accusation can be effectively employed against God's people. Likewise, reviewing the Jewish response to these letters will assist us in learning how to thwart the enemy's efforts through this evil device.

### False Accusations to Darius

Although the Jews had laid the foundation of the temple in 535 BC, the persistent opposition slowed its construction to a grinding halt (Ezra 5:4-5). Fifteen years later God moved two prophets, Haggai and Zechariah, to confront the sins of the people, to confirm their divine chastening and necessity of their repentance.

After Haggai delivered his first message in August 520 BC, the work on the temple resumed. This, of course, was noticed by the enemy who quickly attempted to counter the progress. The temple would stand for a testimony of God in the region, and Satan hates such things. He chose to use the device of threatening accusations, and these would come from the top political figure of the region, Tattenai (Ezra 5:3). Shethar-Bozenai

## The Evil Nexus

and other Tattenai officials approached Zerubbabel and Joshua to ask who had authorized the temple-building project and to request a list of names of those chiefly responsible for the effort (Ezra 5:4). History records that there was unrest throughout the Persian Empire at the time Darius took the throne. Perhaps Tattenai thought that the Jews would, by building their temple, incite rebellion in his region. How did the Jews respond to this attack? They briefly stated a pure testimony of the truth, including the reason the temple had been destroyed in the first place, but they continued working:

> *We are the servants of the God of heaven and earth, and we are rebuilding the temple that was built many years ago, which a great king of Israel built and completed. But because our fathers provoked the God of heaven to wrath, He gave them into the hand of Nebuchadnezzar king of Babylon, the Chaldean, who destroyed this temple and carried the people away to Babylon. However, in the first year of Cyrus king of Babylon, King Cyrus issued a decree to build this house of God* (Ezra 5:11-13).

After hearing this response, governor Tattenai and key political figures drafted a letter to King Darius, informing him of the situation and the Jewish answer, and requesting him to search the Babylonian archives to confirm whether the Jews were indeed finishing the task originally authorized by King Cyrus some eighteen years earlier. Tattenai was inferring that the Jews were lying and had their own agenda and thus should be stopped. Under Persian law the decrees of kings could not be reversed (Dan. 6:12), meaning that if the Jews were telling the truth, their opposition could not force the Jews to stop building the temple. It would take several months to receive a response from King Darius; in the meantime, the Jews continued erecting God's house in Jerusalem. In response to the accusation, God's people simply stated the truth, and kept to the Lord's work. They did not waste time providing a lengthy defense, nor were

# #2 False Accusations

they bullied into halting the construction project in order to pacify the opposition. As a result, King Darius did investigate the matter and bestowed the Jews with abundant resources to finish the work that Cyrus had previously commanded for them to complete, which they did without further hindrance.

## False Accusations to Artaxerxes

The letter to Artaxerxes was penned by Rehum, the chancellor, and Shimshai, his secretary, on behalf of a large contingency of various peoples throughout the region who were adamantly opposed to the Jews rebuilding Jerusalem. This letter contained several false accusations and was successful in causing King Artaxerxes to command that the reconstruction of Jerusalem be halted until further notice. Why were the accusations of Tattenai defeated, but yet Rehum's effort was successful? In short, Rehum incorporated a different strategy into his assault, which Tattenai did not use. A review of Rehum's letter reveals several insidious tactics which were effective in gaining a victory over the Jews.

First, Rehum informed Artaxerxes that the Jews were rebuilding Jerusalem as a fortified city (Ezra 4:11-16): *"Let it be known to the king that the Jews who came up from you have come to us at Jerusalem, and are building the rebellious and evil city, and are finishing its walls and repairing the foundations"* (Ezra 4:12). This statement was clearly false, as the walls of Jerusalem still laid waste when Nehemiah arrived in Jerusalem years later. Lying and accusing are natural to the Father of Lies, the true author of Rehum's letter.

While it is true that the Jews had previously rebelled against the Babylonians, there was no hint of an uprising against the crown of Persia at this time. Yet, the intent of the letter was to plant suspicion in the king's mind through an exaggerated story and the suggestion that if the Jews had a fortified city, they would cease from paying taxes and tribute money to the empire (Ezra 4:13). This, of course, would bring dishonor upon the king's good name (Ezra 4:14). Furthermore, with a stronghold

## The Evil Nexus

in Palestine, the Jews might try to reclaim their land taken by Babylon years earlier. If this occurred, it would weaken the control of the Persian Empire in that region.

After receiving Rehum's letter, King Artaxerxes commanded that the archives be searched for historical information concerning the Jewish people; he wanted to assess whether or not the Jews truly posed a threat to his kingdom. It was learned that Jerusalem had previously been the capital of a powerful kingdom, probably referring to the days of David and Solomon. Artaxerxes decided not to take a chance and wrote the following to the governing authorities in Palestine: *"Now give the command to make these men cease, that this city may not be built until the command is given by me"* (Ezra 4:21). Although the work was forcibly stopped, there were two aspects of Artaxerxes's response which must have encouraged the Jews. First, he acknowledged that they indeed had once been a powerful people, and second, the opportunity for the work to continue in the future was still a possibility. In fact, a few years later Artaxerxes himself would give Nehemiah permission to rebuild the wall of Jerusalem (Neh. 2).

The enemies of the Jews used the same tactic of threatening accusations that had failed during the reign of Darius to stop the work during the reign of his grandson Artaxerxes. Why were the accusations against the Jews effective in stopping the rebuilding of Jerusalem, but not the rebuilding of the temple? Three reasons are suggested. First, the rebuilding of the temple was prophesied in Scripture, and thus, commanded and completed by God in accordance with His sovereign purpose. The effort to rebuild Jerusalem, while noble, was not commanded by God; in fact, God planned to accomplish something quite spectacular at a later day through the leadership of Nehemiah. What had been attempted for decades would be completed in only fifty-two days. Even the enemies of the Jews would recognize that by the hand of Jehovah, the God of the Jews, the impossible had been accomplished (Neh. 6:16).

## #2 False Accusations

A second possible reason that the tactic of accusation worked in the latter case is that the accusers had banded together in greater numbers (Ezra 4:9); it was only the local governor and a few of his companions who wrote to Darius in opposition to the reconstruction of the temple (Ezra 5:6). The appeal to Artaxerxes against the reconstruction of Jerusalem was made by a broad coalition of various people groups throughout the region.

The third reason that the enemy's accusations prospered in the days of Artaxerxes is that what was said about the Jews' history was partly true, although the projected outcome of their labors was not. Through the power of suggestion, the enemy appealed to the king's imagination as to what might happen if the Jews continued their work. During the days of King Darius, the opposition did not believe that the Jews were telling the truth, and therefore they asked the king to validate their claims. They were hoping that Darius would find that the Jews were lying and did not have authority to rebuild the temple. But this was not the case; the Jews were telling the truth and the construction effort continued. However, in the days of Artaxerxes the enemy drew fragments of the truth and embellished the facts to create a false reality. As Eve learned in the Garden of Eden, Satan is particularly dangerous when he combines some degree of truth within his presentation and then misguides his audience by suggesting an untrue outcome, while all the time appealing to self-focused behavior. His attack on her was methodical and deadly. The Jews in the days of Artaxerxes also learned how accusations partly founded in truth are the most dangerous.

### Summary

If we become satisfied with the goodness of God's blessings and yet lose sight of what He desires for us, we will become feeble and powerless – God strengthens those who want to be guided into further knowledge of Himself and the purposes of His grace. Accordingly, Paul exhorts the believers at Colossae to have a faith fully grounded on Christ and His teachings:

# The Evil Nexus

*Now this I say lest anyone should deceive you with persuasive words. For though I am absent in the flesh, yet I am with you in spirit, rejoicing to see your good order and the steadfastness of your faith in Christ. As you therefore have received Christ Jesus the Lord, so walk in Him, rooted and built up in Him and established in the faith, as you have been taught, abounding in it with thanksgiving* (Col. 2:4-7).

God is a God of absolute truth; therefore, let our faith rest on the foundation of biblical truth. If so grounded, we will be less likely to fall prey to threatening accusations and secular reasoning. The value of our service relates directly with having fellowship with God in spirit and in truth (John 4:23). Believers will experience the most satisfaction and joy in life when they are fully resting in God's grace and obeying His Word. In the eternal purposes of God, the accusations of the devil cannot overcome those who abide in the Lord Jesus Christ!

The author has observed that in most confrontational matters the guilty party is the individual who defends himself or herself by gathering others (often friends and family) to accuse the other party of wrongdoing. Neutral seasoned brethren are not sought to resolve such matters to ensure one's self-focused agenda is preserved and accountability for sin is avoided. This was Rehum's effective strategy to overcome the Jews. On the other hand, the individual who leaves the matter with the Lord to judge is usually the innocent party (1 Pet. 2:19-21). Those who choose this course of action are demonstrating true brokenness before the Lord, writes William MacDonald:

> It is a mark of deepest and truest humility to see ourselves condemned without cause and to be silent under it. To be silent under insult and wrong is a very noble imitation of our Lord. "Oh, my Lord, when I remember in how many ways You did suffer, who in no way deserved it, I know not where my senses are when I am in such haste to defend and excuse myself. Is it possible I should desire anyone to speak any

## #2 False Accusations

good of me or to think it, when so many ill things were thought and spoken of You?"[2]

Sometimes even tears, as in the case of profane Esau, can be misleading – embracing an appeal of sympathy apart from reason will often leave us holding hands with the devil. Believers must be motivated by genuine love (i.e., what is in the best interest of others), rather than mere pity (i.e., sympathy apart from reason). This was certainly the case with the Lord Jesus Christ, who was accused of wrongdoing by an emotionally charged crowd, yet He was completely innocent of the charges against Him. He endured the offense patiently:

> *For what credit is it if, when you are beaten for your faults, you take it patiently? But when you do good and suffer, if you take it patiently, this is commendable before God. For to this you were called, because Christ also suffered for us, leaving us an example, that you should follow His steps: "Who committed no sin, Nor was deceit found in His mouth"; who, when He was reviled, did not revile in return; when He suffered, He did not threaten, but committed Himself to Him who judges righteously* (1 Pet. 2:20-23).

The one engaged in social politics and soliciting the aid of others through sympathy is usually the one at the root of the problem. Satan enjoys using such a one to sow division among the brethren instead of making for peace and allowing the Lord to judge the matter. God hates *"a false witness who speaks lies, and one who sows discord among brethren"* (Prov. 6:19). Conversely, those who are wrongly treated but wait patiently and quietly upon the Lord receive a blessing from Him. The next time you are falsely accused, just remember that your accuser has handed you an opportunity to be blessed by the Lord, that is, depending on how you respond. *He who is of a proud heart stirs up strife, but he who trusts in the Lord will be prospered* (Prov. 28:25). For this reason, a believer who understands the eternal aspects of the offense can turn to his or her accuser and say, "Thank you for the blessing which is to come."

## The Christian Response to Accusations

Threatening accusations are like shifting shadows; they can scare us, but they cannot hurt us. The Jews knew *"that the eye of their God was watching over them"* (Ezra 5:5) and by His enablement their enemies would not prevail against them. Their authority came from One who was higher than Tattenai, as validated by the phrase *"the God of Israel, who was over them"* (Ezra 5:1). This expression and others, such as *"the hand of the Lord was on him,"* are found often in the books of Ezra and Nehemiah to confirm that God was present among and co-laboring with His people.

Paul reminds the believers at Corinth of this same truth (1 Cor. 3:9). It is one thing to know God is omnipresent; it is quite another to have His abiding presence and to appreciate His handiwork in all that you do – the Creator and Sustainer of all things is quite able to judge evildoers and deliver the righteous from their tormentors (2 Pet. 2:4-8). Remembering that the one who rules the universe has permitted the offense for His glory and for your edification will enhance your wherewithal to suffer through the situation with joy and to wait patiently for deliverance.

If the Jews had continued working from the onset, the temple would have been finished and no accusations would have been raised against them. But, since they had stopped building for fifteen years, and begun again, it seemed like the Jews were acting on their own authority, not a Persian decree. The lesson to learn from this is to keep busy in the Lord's work. Believers who faithfully co-labor with the Lord will find that they have little time available for the "fluff of life," or for compromising situations which tempt them to sin or invite the allegations of others. It is good for us to remember that the Lord's eye is upon us also; may we continue to co-labor with Him.

# #2 False Accusations

Like the discouraged Jews who stopped building the temple, those with a degraded estimation of God will usually live defeated lives because they also underestimate the strength of the devil and the danger his cunning devices pose. These spiritually despondent souls fall prey to the whims of the enemy, and then fail to learn from their disappointing experiences and rise in grace to victory. Whether we tumble or stumble, it is wise to learn from our blunders. Past failures should not hinder Christians from pressing onward in their heavenly calling. Falling is a normal part of learning to walk properly; it is not falling that makes us a failure, but rather, it is remaining down after the fall: *"A righteous man may fall seven times and rise again, but the wicked shall fall by calamity"* (Prov. 24:16). Dear believer, when you fall, learn from your mistake, get back up in the strength of the Lord, and keep running! There are just consequences for falling, but there are even more for wallowing in self-pity and rejecting God's grace in time of need.

The Lord Jesus was often criticized by the same pharisaical spirit at work in the world today. This self-exalting spirit morphs moral absolutes, the truth, and sound logic into a virtual reality which only suits its master, or those under its influence. The Lord did not waste time defending Himself against this hypocritical influence, but He did, on rare occasions, attempt to reason with those under its power (e.g. Luke 22:52-53; John 18:22-23). There is no suitable defense against someone controlled by a critical spirit – even the glory of God is transformed into evil.

Nothing will satisfy this mindset which tends to visualize a negative reality of the facts. Generally speaking, it is those who do the least who criticize those doing the most. Those who struggle with envy and pride are usually the first in line to speak their mind and the last to change it when the truth is known. Individuals with a predisposed ill-will towards you will be most eager to hop on the bandwagon and then not get off until they are exhausted from beating the dead horse hitched to it. Just expect such irritations in the Lord's work and keep serving the

# The Evil Nexus

One who knows all about false accusations. Time will prove out the truth, but our exhibited humility during such times will speak louder than any evidence of the truth could. It is not our defense which is needful at such times, but rather our surrender to God of the situation. Also, remember to thank the Lord for those who loved you enough to contact you and hear the whole matter out before foolishly receiving gossip or a one-sided story as fact (Prov. 18:13; 1 Cor. 13:5).

Meaningless accusations and unjust criticisms have keenly wounded many Christians and neutralized many profitable ministries. Remembering that Satan, as shown in Scripture, has used these tactics previously to oppose God's work is helpful. If you are doing anything for the Lord, expect to be criticized. Criticism often originates from those unburdened in ministry who unfortunately have the extra time to burden you in yours. Evaluate criticism for potential constructive benefits, especially when it comes from those who love you unquestionably, and then cast the rest aside and forget about it. If you are prompted to critique someone else, know that if it pains you to do so, then you have the right attitude, but if you have even a hint of pleasure in the matter, then it would be best to keep still. Why? This is because our flesh naturally opposes the things of God (Gal. 5:17), and *"the wrath of man does not produce the righteousness of God"* (Jas. 1:20). Paul did not even judge the value of his own ministry because he knew his flesh was biased (1 Cor. 4:2-4). A spiritual person wants to edify others, not hurt them for the sake of personal vindication or self-justification.

As the Jews soon learned, living for God and doing what pleases Him often has a dire consequence – suffering. Paul reminded his spiritual son Timothy of this important fact: *"Yes, and all who desire to live godly in Christ Jesus will suffer persecution"* (2 Tim. 3:12). This is a facet of the Christian experience for which all believers need to be mentally prepared (1 Pet. 1:13), and in which they ought to rejoice (Acts 5:40-42, 16:23-25). Paul told the saints at both Philippi and Thessalonica, who were being persecuted for their faith, that suffering patiently

## #2 False Accusations

was evidence (a proof) of their salvation (Phil. 1:28; 2 Thess. 1:5).

The Jews who returned from Babylonian captivity were suffering patiently in the will of God and He was blessing their work in a tremendous way. When living for Christ becomes arduous, let us remember that it is God and not our accusers who control the worth of our service! When accusations come, attend to your character and allow God to protect your reputation as He deems best: *"The Lord rewarded me according to my righteousness; according to the cleanness of my hands He has recompensed me"* (Ps. 18:20). Ability usually rises to prominence, but without good character all will be lost. These are school days and God must bring us to the end of ourselves before we can be fully profitable to Him. Perhaps A. W. Tozer expresses this point best: "It is doubtful whether God can bless a man greatly until He has hurt him deeply."

**Meditation**

> Abraham Lincoln once said, "If I tried to read, much less answer, all the criticisms made of me, and all the attacks leveled against me, this office would have to be closed for all other business. I do the best I know how, the very best I can. And I mean to keep on doing this, down to the very end. If the end brings me out all wrong, ten angels swearing I had been right would make no difference. If the end brings me out all right, then what is said against me now will not amount to anything."[3]

> If what they are saying about you is true, mend your ways. If it isn't true, forget it, and go on and serve the Lord.
>
> — H. A. Ironside

> I have known the pain of betrayal and of criticism, much of it justified and the rest sanctified.
> — William MacDonald

# #3 Slander

Paul established moral and spiritual criteria for recognizing church leaders (i.e. elders) and deacons in his first epistle to Timothy. When addressing the appointment of deacons, he indicates that their wives, who presumably may help support their husbands in that role, must *"be reverent, not slanderers, temperate, faithful in all things"* (1 Tim. 3:11). The Greek word *diabolos* is normally translated "devil," but is rendered "slanderer" in this verse. In the previous chapter it was noted that *diabolos* was translated as "false accusers." The English word "slander" is also translated from the Greek word *dibbah*, which means "to defame or give an evil (unrighteous) report." Thus, to accuse the innocent of wrongdoing or to slander another's just character is devilish behavior which bestows honor to Satan, not the Lord Jesus Christ. The Lord moreover implies that such insults are a form of murder:

> *You have heard that it was said to those of old, "You shall not murder, and whoever murders will be in danger of the judgment." But I say to you that whoever is angry with his brother without a cause shall be in danger of the judgment. And whoever says to his brother, "Raca!" shall be in danger of the council* (Matt. 5:21-22).

"Raca" was an Aramaic term meaning "empty one." When spoken in rage or in resentment towards another, it was understood as a term of utter reproach, suggesting that the recipient was "totally worthless." The Lord was highlighting that such destructive insults had the same moral effect as thrusting a

## The Evil Nexus

dagger into another's heart, and thus, was considered a form of murder that would be severely judged. All Christians have significance to the Lord and it is not our place to devalue others through slander. The devil was a murderer from the beginning of man's existence and our slander against others merely mimics his behavior. Yet, children of God are not to be "little devils," that is, engaging in what God detests, and the devil incites.

### A Historical Example

The devil does not bother with halfhearted believers, but once they become desperate for God and burdened for the work of God, he will intensify his opposition against them. Those with mental strongholds of hatred, bitterness, anger, jealousy, and pride will be easy targets of the devil's solicitations to join ranks with him in order to confront and discourage those the Lord is using. Scripture shows that this devilish nexus has been repeatedly employed to confront various works of God. Satan hates that which is precious to the Lord, namely, a testimony of His greatness through His people.

For example, Jerusalem was and will be the center of God's earthly purposes for His covenant people. Thus, Satan opposed the rebuilding of the wall around Jerusalem in Nehemiah's time and withstood the reconstruction of the temple in Zerubbabel's day. The books of Nehemiah and Ezra reveal that the severity of his opposition increased proportionately with the resolve of God's people to labor for Him; thus intense slander was inevitable.

The chief enemy of the Jews in Nehemiah's day was Sanballat the Horonite. He was deeply grieved after hearing that Nehemiah had come from Shushan to seek the welfare of the Jews (Neh. 2:10). He despised the Jews and derided them in an attempt to sidetrack them from starting the building project after Nehemiah had rallied the people to do so (Neh. 2:19). Later, he was enraged by the news that the Jews had actually begun to clear debris and repair the wall. However, all of his ridicule and mocking did not weaken Jewish resolve to rise and build (Neh.

## #3 Slander

4:1). Sanballat then resorted to discouraging the Jews from building by terrorizing them (Neh. 4:11-12). Yet, Jehovah was laboring among His people, and though the enemy incited fear, nothing came of his threats.

Besides Sanballat, the other ringleaders of the Jewish opposition were Tobiah and Geshem. No doubt every move within the city was being reported to them; accordingly, they must have enjoyed the news that internal strife among the Jews, recorded in Nehemiah 5, had delayed the construction project. The probable reason the narrative in that chapter does not mention them is that if God's people get quarrelling among themselves, their enemies can afford to relax in their tents. However, as soon as unity among believers is restored, the adversary is quickly aroused to engage in the conflict again.

Having failed to slow the Jews' progress, the enemies would now concentrate their attack on the one who had inspired the Jews to do what they thought was an impossible enterprise. They were desperate; Nehemiah must be stopped at all costs – only then could this well-managed construction project become disorganized. The strategy, simply put, was "stop the leader to stop the work." The attack would focus on God's leadership and be the enemy's final attempt to stop the completion of the wall. Dear beloved, pray for your church leaders, for they will be prone to recurring attacks of slander, false accusations, and solicitations to do evil. Satan knows that if he can cause the undershepherds of the local assembly to fall, he can destroy the testimony that God has raised for Himself in a community.

Nehemiah 6:1 states that the wall was nearly finished; all breaches have been repaired, but the gates have not yet been placed; time was running out for the opposition. The enemy mounted a desperate four-pronged assault against Nehemiah in a final attempt to halt the building project. Accordingly, Nehemiah 6 supplies one of the best portions of Scripture to analyze the devilish tactic of slander and its objective: to discourage and defocus God's people.

## The Evil Nexus

First, the enemy repeatedly solicited Nehemiah to withdraw from the safety of his Jewish comrades to discuss the situation. Nehemiah rejected each invitation with the same concise and trite response: *"I am doing a great work, so that I cannot come down. Why should the work cease while I leave it and go down to you?"* (Neh. 6:3). He knew what the Lord wanted him to do, and it did not include abandoning the work of God to dialogue with children of the devil.

The second strategy against Nehemiah was to slander him and then accuse him of wrongdoing through an open letter (Neh. 6:5). The enemy hoped that Nehemiah might want to avoid a scandal and thereby accept their cordial invitation to discuss the matter privately and then be immediately terminated. If this was not possible, the enemy hoped to at least cast doubt on Nehemiah's character by publicly criticizing and discrediting him.

> People who are constantly criticizing others are usually guilty of something worse in their own lives.
>
> — Warren Weirsbe

It was suggested in the "open letter" that Nehemiah wanted to be king of the Jews and was only building the wall to protect his kingship (Neh. 6:6). It was further suggested that he would appoint prophets to speak on his behalf in order to coerce the people into blindly following him (Neh. 6:7). These accusations cast Nehemiah as a self-seeking, power-hungry man who was secretly plotting treason against Artaxerxes. What was Nehemiah's response? He denied the accusation flatly and told his adversaries that they had quite an imagination; he then committed himself to God through prayer (Neh. 6:8-9). Harry Ironside contrasts Nehemiah's response with the agenda of his adversaries:

> Nehemiah is not at all concerned about this. He knows he is personally right with God and he fears not suspicion and idle

## #3 Slander

tales. "There are no such things done as you say," he retorts boldly, "but you feigned them out of your own heart." So was it also when evil workers sought to undermine the apostle Paul's influence, and so has it ever been when the truth was hated. To discredit, by fair means or foul, the messenger is one of Satan's cunning devices in order to discredit the message. To do this, his tools often affect great humility themselves; and pretending to be zealous for the liberty of the people of God, they cry "Pope!" "Diotrephes!" "Heretic!" when any servant of Christ and the Church seeks to stand steadfastly against iniquity. They hope to thereby throw dust in the eyes of simple believers, in order to gain their own unrighteous ends. Trials like these are not easy to bear. To have one's good evil-spoken of, to be called a "lord over God's heritage" when trying to serve in lowliness, is painful indeed to any sensitive soul. But it is well not to retaliate, nor even to explain, but just to refuse the cowardly charge and leave results with God.[1]

Thankfully this despicable tactic did not work; Nehemiah did not heed the enemy's insinuations, but rather, he continued doing what God had assigned him. The enemy then tried to assassinate Nehemiah through the false prophesying of a Jew named Shemaiah, who tried to lure Nehemiah to hide with him in the temple. Shemaiah had been paid by Sanballat and Tobiah to betray Nehemiah in this way (Neh. 6:10-12). Nehemiah knew that the Law permitted only the priests to venture into the temple's sanctuary (Num. 3:10, 18:7). He was thus forbidden to hide there. Knowing that God would not contradict Himself, Nehemiah rightly discerned that Shemaiah was not speaking for God and Nehemiah's life was saved.

Despite the enemy's attempts to snuff out the life of Nehemiah through solicitation, slander, and treachery, Nehemiah was preserved and led his people to accomplish one of the greatest feats recorded in the Bible. Jerusalem's wall and its gates were built in just fifty-two days (Neh. 6:15). What effect did this achievement have on the enemy? Nehemiah tells us: *"And it*

# The Evil Nexus

*happened, when all our enemies heard of it, and all the nations around us saw these things, that they were very disheartened in their own eyes; for they perceived that this work was done by our God"* (Neh. 6:16). Despite the wiles of the enemy, the wall was finished and thus supplied a testimony of God's greatness for all to witness. Even the opposition, seeing what a people so outwardly weak had accomplished in the presence of an enemy so strong, was forced to admit *"this work was done by the God of the Jews."*

The monumental feat was a bitter-sweet experience for Nehemiah, because the enemy continued to oppose him even after the city was secure. The fourth type of attack mentioned against Nehemiah in this chapter is treason from his own people (Neh. 6:17-18). It is often after a great victory has been achieved that Satan does his worst damage. Believers, wearied after a laborious undertaking, feel that they deserve a break, some downtime to relax. Having let down their guard, the enemy's movements go undetected until it is too late. Yes, in the Lord, Nehemiah had accomplished a tremendous victory, but he had not earned a vacation. Likewise, the spiritual foes battling the believer never sleep. Believers must always stand ready and be vigilant against potential attack.

## Summary

Being unable to stop the wall-building effort, the enemy shifted its focus from the people to their leader. Besides several assassination attempts on Nehemiah's life, both from within and without Jewish ranks, the enemy slandered him and accused him of wrongdoing through an open letter. Nehemiah's response to these tactics should prompt us to be spiritually alert for false brethren, to trust in God's Word for direction, to pray for deliverance when attacked, to ignore slander and keep doing the Lord's work, and to remember that Satan often assaults believers directly after their accomplishments.

It was Nehemiah's unwavering faith in Jehovah and his irreproachable character that enabled him to undertake amazing

## #3 Slander

feats for God. It is emphasized that the revealed character of the servant of God is as important as what that servant does. The servant of the Lord represents God in character and conduct; neither aspect can be missing from a true testimony of God. As a result of Nehemiah's resolve and leadership, the enemies of the Jews were forced to hang their heads and acknowledge Jehovah. The wall was a reminder to the Jews that God was with them. It would also serve as a testimony to the surrounding nations that the one true God resided in Jerusalem and dwelled among His people. Lastly, the wall would be a constant reminder to the opposition of their defeat (Neh. 6:16). There is much to be gained when God's people revive, rise in unity, avoid and die to slander, and build for the Lord!

### The Christian Response to Slander

As shown in the first portion of Nehemiah 6, sometimes the devil breaks down the resolve of the believer to do what he or she knows is right through repeated solicitations; this is especially true when we are isolated from accountability. It is one thing for a child of God to waste time entertaining goats instead of tending to God's sheep, and it is quite another to leave the safety of the sheepfold and to become the prey of ravenous wolves. Thankfully, Nehemiah did neither – he stayed focused on the important task before him, remained in the company of God's people, and ignored the solicitations of the enemy. How many Christians would not have shipwrecked their lives if they would have heeded Nehemiah's example!

No doubt Nehemiah was criticized for not attempting to make peace with his adversaries, but what peace can a child of God and a child of the devil have with each other (2 Cor. 6:14-15)? None! Beware when the enemy says, *"come let us meet together."* The one behind the face of your aggressor is the father of lies, and the Lord Jesus said *"there is no truth in him"* (John 8:44). Dear believer, be discerning; not every religious movement and sympathetic appeal is of God; we must exercise care not to get involved with those who are actually opposing

## The Evil Nexus

the Lord. Expect criticism and slander for refusing to get involved, but this is much more desirable than to become a casualty of war.

> The best way to deal with slander is to pray about it: God will either remove it, or remove the sting from it. Our own attempts at clearing ourselves are usually failures; we are like the boy who wished to remove the blot from his copy, and by his bungling made it ten times worse.
>
> — Charles Spurgeon

Satan was defeated at Calvary (John 12:31) and further humiliated by the resurrection of Christ (Eph. 1:19-21). His only recourse since those events has been to cast doubt upon the work of Christ and to defame His person and character. Satan and his worldly domain hate the Lord Jesus and will go to any extreme to slander Him and those who desire to live for Christ (John 15:18-19). The last thing Satan wants now is people on earth who remind him of Christ and who are doing the will of God – people who are, as Nehemiah put it, *"true servants of the Lord"* (Neh. 1:11). Abraham Lincoln provides us with a good example as how to respond when others slander:

> During the administration of Lincoln, a delegation from a western state called upon him with a written protest against a certain appointment. In particular the paper had a list of specific objections against a Senator Baker, a longtime and beloved friend of the president. The objections were definite reflections on Baker's character. Holding the paper in his hand, Lincoln asked with calm dignity: "This is my paper which you have given me?" When they assured him that it was, he asked further: "To do with as I please?" "Certainly, Mr. President," replied the spokesman. Lincoln leaned over to the fireplace, laid the paper on the hot coals, turned to the group and said: "Good day, gentlemen."[2]

## #3 Slander

To protect those whom Christ loves from the damage of slander, may we too have the courage to say, "Good day, gentlemen." Believers should completely abstain from slandering others; it is the devil's work to discredit honorable servants and to cast doubt on their character. To do so robs the accused party of what is precious and ultimately brings harm to the accuser. When slandered, simply state the truth as Nehemiah did, but do not waste time defending yourself, otherwise the work of God will be neglected. If Satan can solicit a believer to be self-protecting rather than to commit himself or herself into the Lord's care, the enemy wins a victory. How can this be, you may ask? When time is wasted, the Lord's work is ignored, and self-sufficiency displaces grace-sufficiency – Satan gains a check in the win column.

Throughout the wall-building experience, the Jews learned that the insults, the threatenings, the accusations, and the slander were merely flittering shadows which faded with the setting sun. Shadows may scare us, but they have no power to hurt anyone. It is only when we have a diminished opinion of God that the enemy's suggestions (or shadows) gain a foothold in our minds. Dear believer, do not allow anyone to rob your joy. Happiness depends on what happens, but rejoicing with a clear conscious is a tremendous blessing and thus a wise choice.

> No flattery can heal a bad conscience, so no slander can hurt a good one.
> — Thomas Watson

Though Paul was incarcerated in Rome for preaching Christ, and though his opponents were aggressively preaching against him, he found something in his situation to rejoice in – weak believers were boldly preaching Christ because he was suffering faithfully for Christ. Instead of complaining, Paul set his mind on praising God for the positive things God was accomplishing despite his circumstances: *"in this I rejoice, yes, and will rejoice"* (Phil. 1:18). There is always something for which we can

## The Evil Nexus

rejoice no matter how dire the situation – find it and hang on to it. In such troubling times, let us maintain an unwavering confidence in the character of God despite our circumstances and the joy of the Lord will be ours!

## Meditation

David was a man after God's own heart, and accordingly was acquainted with betrayal, slander, false accusations, and discouragement. He acknowledges that his sufficiency was in the Lord alone:

> *With the pure You will show Yourself pure; and with the devious You will show Yourself shrewd* (Ps. 18:26).

> *The Lord is near to those who have a broken heart, and saves such as have a contrite spirit. Many are the afflictions of the righteous, but the Lord delivers him out of them all* (Ps. 34:18-19).

> *Let those be put to shame and brought to dishonor who seek after my life; let those be turned back and brought to confusion who plot my hurt* (Ps. 35:4).

> *Rest in the Lord, and wait patiently for Him; do not fret because of him who prospers in his way, because of the man who brings wicked schemes to pass* (Ps. 37:7).

John Bunyan, who suffered years of imprisonment in England during the seventeenth century for preaching Christ, found that his joy in life rested in the sufficiency of Christ and through completely identifying with Him:

> Therefore, I bind these lies and slanderous accusations to my person as an ornament; it belongs to my Christian profession to be vilified, slandered, reproached and reviled, and since all this is nothing but that, as God and my conscience testify, I rejoice in being reproached for Christ's sake.[3]

# #4 Strife and Division

James ties strife and division with the work of the devil: *"For where envying and strife is, there is confusion and every evil work"* (Jas. 3:16; KJV). On the other hand, the unity of God's people is precious to Him: *"Behold, how good and how pleasant it is for brethren to dwell together in unity!"* (Ps. 133:1). In fact, unity within the Church is something that the Holy Spirit is constantly working to achieve; unfortunately our proud behavior often opposes His efforts (Eph. 4:3). The inescapable consequence of grieving Him is powerless ministry and spiritual dryness.

## Unity is God's Work

The first time Joshua attacked Ai, he did so in his own wisdom and strength; he did not consult the Lord before sending his troops into battle (Josh. 7:1-5). He reasoned that because Ai was a smaller city than Jericho, three thousand soldiers would be more than sufficient to conquer it. The battle was a disaster, thirty-six Jews perished; this would be their worst defeat during the entire seven-year military campaign in Canaan. Through that loss the Lord taught Joshua the woeful ramifications of engaging the enemy in the power of the flesh and the importance of unity among God's people in His work – all of the Israelite army would later be sent to conquer Ai. After Achan's sin had been properly dealt with, Jehovah was again present with His people in their warfare and Ai was completely conquered with no Jewish fatalities (Josh. 8).

Nehemiah realized the necessity of involving all the people in the work of rebuilding the wall about Jerusalem, for the task was enormous. So he sought the cooperation of the people and

## The Evil Nexus

committed himself to co-labor with them: *"Let us rise up and build"* (Neh. 2:18). Though the opposition was fierce, unity of purpose enabled the Lord's people to stand as one with Him and be unconquerable.

Moses also highlighted the importance of unity and working with God: *"How could one chase a thousand, and two put ten thousand to flight, unless their Rock had sold them, and the Lord had surrendered them?"* (Deut. 32:30). God can use one man to defeat a thousand foes, but two men fighting as one with the Lord can defeat ten thousand!

The first five chapters of Acts indicate that the early Church was successful in evangelism when there was unity and Christ-mindedness among the disciples. When there were division and factions within the church, their testimony was marred, the Spirit was quenched, and fruitfulness ceased (Acts 6:1-6). Yet, as soon as unity among the brethren was again achieved we read: *"Then the word of God spread, and the number of the disciples multiplied greatly in Jerusalem, and a great many of the priests were obedient to the faith"* (Acts 6:7). What is the lesson to be learned? Believers must lay hold of the mind of Christ to remain in unity. As before mentioned, the Holy Spirit works to maintain unity among believers, but believers must labor to keep it (Eph. 4:3). This is accomplished by humbling ourselves and putting the interest of others ahead of our own. A busybody inserts his or her interests into the affairs of others, but a Christ-minded believer puts the welfare of others above his or her own interests – this type of attitude ends strife.

Having the mind of Christ ensures unity among His people and that they are doing *"all to the glory of God"* (1 Cor. 10:31). On the eve of His suffering, the Lord repeatedly acknowledged in His prayer in John 17 the inseparable link between unity and the display of the glory of God:

> *I do not pray for these alone, but also for those who will believe in Me through their word; that they all may be one, as You, Father, are in Me, and I in You; that they also may be*

## #4 Strife and Division

*one in Us, that the world may believe that You sent Me. And the glory which You gave Me I have given them, that they may be one just as We are one: I in them, and You in Me; that they may be made perfect in one, and that the world may know that You have sent Me, and have loved them as You have loved Me* (John 17:20-23).

When the Church is unified, the glory of a triune God, who is always in unity, is displayed for all to witness. Peaceful unity and loving-kindness among men is not a naturally occurring phenomenon, so when it does transpire the world takes notice (John 13:35). The lost are prompted to consider what they see and by the grace of God some will be won to Christ! It is absolutely necessary for a local assembly to be of one accord before they can properly exhibit Christ to their neighborhoods. If there is disunity in the local church, the work of the Holy Spirit is concentrated within the house of God in order to remove the rubble of pride, hypocrisy, willful sin, and doctrinal error. When the flesh-controlled operations are removed from the local assembly, then Spirit-controlled saints will rise up together and be more than conquerors for the glory of God. Let us all remember that *"it is honorable for a man to stop striving, since any fool can start a quarrel* (Prov. 20:3).

## Summary

As in the days of Moses, Joshua, and Nehemiah, Satan continues presently to oppose any true testimony of God's character and nature as established in gatherings of His people (i.e. assemblies of Christians). Today, it is not a temple or a wall that manifests the manifold wisdom of God, but the Church: *"To the intent that now the manifold wisdom of God might be made known by the church to the principalities and powers in the heavenly places, according to the eternal purpose which He accomplished in Christ Jesus our Lord"* (Eph. 3:10-11). It should then be no surprise that when a local church becomes burdened to remove the debris of religious pride, carnality, disunity, and

# The Evil Nexus

spiritual slothfulness from their midst in order to erect a true testimony for Christ, the enemy will intensely seek to thwart the rebuilding program.

A notable example of this fact is contained in one of the oldest books of the Bible – the book of Job. Job was a God-fearing man who led his family in unified worship. One day when Satan had to present himself before God's throne in heaven, the Lord said to him, *"Have you considered My servant Job, that there is none like him on the earth, a blameless and upright man, one who fears God and shuns evil?"* (Job 1:8). God furnished a glowing character sketch of Job, whom He considered His righteous servant. The proclamation brought an immediate challenge from Satan who was allowed by God to initiate a series of horrendous circumstances to test Job's wherewithal. In the end, Job was greatly honored and blessed, and God was exalted before Satan. Likewise, Christ-centered unity among God's people will certainly invite a challenge from the enemy to destroy it.

## The Christian Response to Strife and Divisions

Solomon reminds us of two realities concerning division among God's people. First, God intensely loathes those who sow discord among His people (Prov. 6:19). Second, pride is a primary fountainhead from which strife springs: *"By pride comes nothing but strife, but with the well-advised is wisdom"* (Prov. 13:10). Pondering this verse, Harry A. Ironside suggests:

> It is an old saying that "it takes two to make a quarrel." Contention begins when the effort to maintain a foolish dignity prevails, or the heart covets what belongs to another. The strife soon ceases when the offended one meets his offender in lowliness and grace. Wisdom enables the well-advised to give the soft answer that turns away wrath.[1]

All the disunity and contention within the Church today is the result of our pride in one form or another. Nothing good can

## #4 Strife and Division

come from pride! This is why Paul admonished the believers at Philippi to follows Christ's example of selfless humility: *"Let nothing be done through strife or vainglory; but in lowliness of mind let each esteem others better than themselves"* (Phil. 2:3; KJV). As R. C. Chapman attests, this is the best defense against the pride that naturally consumes us:

> In 1 Corinthians 15. 28 were read: "Then shall the son also Himself be subject," and in Revelation, "The throne of God and of the Lamb." Christ is forever the Shepherd and forever the Lamb, and it is the lowly or little Lamb, the diminutive being used. There is an infiniteness in the lowliness of the blessed Lamb, and He is now at the utmost of His lowliness. Satan took upon himself the form of a master, being created a servant; instead of serving in obedience he would be lord, and "the condemnation of the devil" is in his self-will; he chose to take to himself what belonged only to God. What a rebuke to the devil the exaltation of the Son of God will be to all eternity – a mirror in which to see his own folly! Acquaintance with the Cross of Christ brings me to nothing! Let any thought of self-exaltation be to me as a serpent; I have nothing to do but to kill it![2]

Strife is the devil's way to get one's way, but lowliness permits God to judge legitimate wrongs His way, which is always the best way. How do we know this is true? Vengeance (i.e., justified wrath for sin) is the Lord's alone (Rom. 12:19); only He can rightly dispense wrath to humble the proud heart (Job 40:11-12) and as previously noted, the wrath of man does not work the righteousness of God (Jas. 1:20). David understood these wrath realities and thus asked the Lord to vindicate him and judge his oppressors; he reckoned that God was much better able to judge his oppressors than he ever could through strife:

> *Plead my cause, O Lord, with those who strive with me; fight against those who fight against me* (Ps. 35:1).

# The Evil Nexus

*Stir up Yourself, and awake to my vindication, to my cause, my God and my Lord. Vindicate me, O Lord my God, according to Your righteousness; and let them not rejoice over me* (Ps. 35:23-24).

We do well to remember that *"God resists the proud, but gives grace to the humble"* (Jas. 4:6). Consequently, our religious pride, condescending attitudes, and fleshly tactics merely insure that God is opposing our endeavors, no matter how lofty we think our intentions are. How can God empower us to serve Him, when we engage in the very behavior He hates – pride and sowing discord among the brethren (Prov. 6:16, 19)?

The Church at Corinth was plagued by petty divisions and hero worship. Some believers had their favorite preachers and were apparently arguing over the matter (1 Cor. 1:12). Paul exhorts them:

> *I plead with you, brethren, by the name of our Lord Jesus Christ, that you all speak the same thing, and that there be no divisions among you, but that you be perfectly joined together in the same mind and in the same judgment* (1 Cor. 1:10).

> *For you are still carnal. For where there are envy, strife, and divisions among you, are you not carnal and behaving like mere men? For when one says, "I am of Paul," and another, "I am of Apollos," are you not carnal?* (1 Cor. 3:3-4).

The divisions among them had resulted because believers had become earthly focused instead of being heavenly minded. Paul calls them "carnal." This church had a number of doctrinal and church order problems, but Paul begins his corrective ministry by affirming the headship of Christ in the Church. In fact, he refers to the Lordship of Christ some six times in the first ten verses of 1 Corinthians. Much of the division within the Church would be resolved if believers kept focused on Christ's manifold perfections and not on the imperfections of others. He is Lord alone, and all other believers have an equal standing as

## #4 Strife and Division

"brethren," a term which includes the "sisteren" (Matt. 23:8; Gal. 3:28). Accordingly, let us not exalt men to a higher rank than what Scripture permits.

> However sweet the word may sound, any sectarian boasting is but the babbling of a babe. The divisions in the Church are due to no other cause than to lack of love and walking after the flesh.
> — Watchman Nee

Believers have different roles within the Church, but none should seek the praise of men, or honorable titles – all epithets and all praise are reserved for the Lord Jesus Christ. John, speaking of Christ, declared the proper obligation of all true believers: *"He must increase, but I must decrease"* (John 3:30). Elihu put the matter this way: *"Let me not, I pray you, accept any man's person, **neither let me give flattering titles unto man**. For I know not to give flattering titles; in so doing my Maker would soon take me away"* (Job 32:21-22; KJV). Men love religious titles, but lovers of Christ should take none – all titles of position in Scripture belong to Him, there is no example of His followers accepting any such honor.

It is understood that some disputes between believers need a wise and godly third party to help sort the problem out (1 Cor. 6:4). After camping at a river near Ahava, Ezra soon learned that he had departed Babylon without any Levites; he sought "men of understanding" to resolve his crisis (Ezra 8:16). Likewise in our distresses, seasoned godly believers can act as peacemakers. The Lord Jesus indicates that there is a special blessing for these individuals, for *"blessed are the peacemakers"* (Matt. 5:9). William MacDonald makes the following observation for this verse:

> Notice that the Lord is not speaking about people with a peaceful disposition or those who love peace. He is referring to those who actively intervene to make peace. The natural approach is to watch strife from the sidelines. The divine

# The Evil Nexus

approach is to take positive action toward creating peace, even if it means taking abuse and invective. ...By making peace, believers manifest themselves as sons of God, and God will one day acknowledge them as people who bear the family likeness.[3]

Blessed are those who can reconcile brethren and achieve unity among God's people. Knowing that God hates disunity among the brethren, and the Holy Spirit's enabling power is quenched at such times, should encourage every believer to relinquish self-rights and fight for the middle ground of peace. This may require a neutral third party to bring biblical clarity to the situation. If unity is not possible, then it is better to part in peace and cease from striving that the work of God may continue. This was the wise determination of Paul and Barnabas concerning their disagreement over John Mark (Acts 15:36-41). In the end, two missionary teams instead of one were sent out, Silas was mentored, and John Mark was restored to profitability. Frankly, our young people do not need to see any more division in the Church, but rather saints that love the Lord and each other enough to receive exhortation graciously, yield personal rights willingly, and choose to serve one another unselfishly. This type of behavior precludes strife and secures the greater good of the Body of Christ.

Though God does not stir up strife among His people, He can certainly overrule its outcome by bestowing vast blessing to more people and also honor to His name in the process. In this way, God manages the outcome of division among His people to affirm who is approved of Him and who is in error (1 Cor. 11:18-19).

## Meditation

Division has done more to hide Christ from the view of men than all the infidelity that has ever been spoken.

— George MacDonald

# #5 Blasphemy

John informs us that Satan has ascribed to himself *"a blasphemous name"* (Rev. 13:1-2) and that his evil representative on earth during the Tribulation Period, the Antichrist, will speak great blasphemies against God (Rev. 13:6). Following the example of his evil authority, the Antichrist will also be identified by many blasphemous names (Rev. 17:3). The devil is a prodigious blasphemer and those who belong to him delight in doing the same!

## What is Blasphemy?

What is blasphemy? Can a Christian honor the devil by blaspheming God? These are important questions, and the Word of God provides answers to each. First, let us examine the meaning of blasphemy, which directly relates to the third of the Ten Commandments that God provided Moses on Mount Sinai: *"You shall not take the name of the Lord your God in vain, for the Lord will not hold him guiltless who takes His name in vain"* (Ex. 20:7). The psalmist reminds us that *"Holy and awesome"* is God's name (Ps. 111:9). Accordingly, God is blasphemed when dishonor is affixed to His name. This can be accomplished in two ways, either by exalting what is common to a high and holy status, or by reckoning what is lofty and divine, such as God's name, to an earthly worth.

Practically speaking, what does obedience to the third of the Ten Commandments entail? How can I know if I am breaking this commandment? Charles Hodge again clarifies the matter for us:

> The third commandment, therefore, specially forbids not only perjury, but also all profane, or unnecessary oaths, all careless

# The Evil Nexus

appeals to God, and all irreverent use of His name. All literature, whether profane or Christian, shows how strong is the tendency in human nature to introduce the name of God even on the most trivial occasions. Not only are those formulas, such as Adieu, Good-bye or God be with you, and God forbid, which may have had a pious origin, constantly used without any recognition of their true import, but even persons professing to fear God often allow themselves to use His name as a mere expression of surprise. God is everywhere present. He hears all we say. He is worthy of the highest reverence; and He will not hold him guiltless who on any occasion uses His name irreverently.[1]

The Old Testament contains several examples of individuals who blasphemed the Lord's name and the consequences they suffered for so doing. One of the most intriguing narratives involving blasphemy relates the occasion where a non-Jewish man, and thus unfamiliar with the Law, is given the death penalty for blaspheming the name of the Lord (Lev. 24:10-23). Leviticus is the worship manual of Israel – it provided the means for God's people to draw near to God through animal sacrifices (i.e. through the shedding and applying of blood). At first glance, one might wonder why the Levitical instruction was interrupted in order to record the fact that a blasphemer was judged, but the event illustrated God's holiness and, therefore, is not an interruption. God was to be reverenced in the land, and not even "strangers" were to blaspheme the name of the God of Israel. Warren Wiersbe explains:

> The basis for obedience to the law is the fear of the Lord, and people who blaspheme His holy name have no fear of God in their hearts. Every Jew knew the third commandment: *"You shall not take the name of the Lord your God in vain, for the Lord will not hold him guiltless who takes His name in vain"* (Ex. 20:7). So fearful were the Jews of breaking this commandment that they substituted the name "Adonai" for "Jehovah" when they read the Scriptures, thus never speaking God's name at all. To respect a name is to respect the person

# #5 Blasphemy

who bears that name, and our highest respect belongs to the Lord.[2]

In the New Testament, the word "blasphemy" appears in both a noun form *blasphemia*, occurring nineteen times, and in a verb form *blasphemeo*, found thirty-five times. *Blasphemia* is translated "blasphemy," "evil speaking," and "railing." It denotes "slander or speech injurious to another's good name (Matt. 12:31) or impious speech disdaining divine majesty (Matt. 26:65)." *Blasphemeo* is rendered "blaspheme" (-er, -mously, -my), "defame," "rail on," "revile," "speak evil." It is the act of "speaking reproachfully, to rail at, or to revile (especially against God)."

It is hard to fathom a day that man has blasphemed his Creator more than that dark day when mankind mocked, spit upon, beat, scourged, and then nailed Him to a cross. Human insurrection surged at the very juncture in time when the precious Savior suffered on humanity's behalf. During this event Scripture applies the Greek *blasphemeo* in the following insults:

> *Now the men who held Jesus mocked Him and beat Him. And having blindfolded Him, they struck Him on the face and asked Him, saying, "Prophesy! Who is the one who struck You?" And many other things they **blasphemously** spoke against Him* (Luke 22:63-65).

> *And those who passed by **blasphemed** Him, wagging their heads and saying, "Aha! You who destroy the temple and build it in three days, save Yourself, and come down from the cross!"* (Mark 15:29-31).

> *Then one of the criminals who were hanged **blasphemed** Him, saying, "If You are the Christ, save Yourself and us"* (Luke 23:39).

The unfathomable grace and mercy of God was thus demonstrated on that day in various ways. First, God the Father

## The Evil Nexus

punished His own Son, the Lord Jesus Christ, for all of humanity's sin and the Savior willingly suffered death in our place in accordance with His Father's will (Heb. 2:9; 1 Jn. 2:2). Second, though the Lord Jesus was blasphemed by the very creatures He was dying for, God the Father took no action to right the wrong, other than to punish His own sinless Son for their crimes. The opportunity of our salvation thus greatly pained the heart of God, for *"He made Him [Christ] who knew no sin, to be sin for us, that we might be made the righteousness of God in Him"* (2 Cor. 5:21).

### Summary

When an individual rails, slanders, or speaks evil against God to cause injury, harm, or offense, that individual has blasphemed God. Specifically applied, the sin of blasphemy involves showing disdain or a lack of reverence for God or for what He deems as sacred (Matt. 26:65), or attributing divine characteristics to something or someone other than God. (The Jews accused Jesus of doing this; see Mark 14:64.) The psalmist sums the matter up concisely – only fools blaspheme the name of God! *"Remember this, that the enemy has reproached, O Lord, and that a foolish people has blasphemed Your name"* (Ps. 74:18).

This psalm contains the plea of God's people for the Lord's help and restoration and for His judgment upon their adversaries who pompously blaspheme the name of the Lord. *"O God, how long will the adversary reproach? Will the enemy blaspheme Your name forever?"* (Ps. 74:10). Matthew Henry provides a splendid devotional thought in conjunction with honoring the name of God:

> As nothing grieves the saints more than to hear God's name blasphemed, so nothing encourages them more to hope that God will appear against their enemies than when they have arrived at such a pitch of wickedness as to reproach God Himself; this fills the measure of their sins apace and hastens

# #5 Blasphemy

their ruin. The psalmist insists much upon this: "We dare not answer their reproaches; Lord, do Thou answer them. Remember that the *foolish people have blasphemed Thy name* and that still *the foolish man reproaches Thee daily.*"' Observe the character of those that reproach God; they are foolish. As atheism is folly (Ps. 14:1), profaneness and blasphemy are no less so.[3]

The foolishness of man is never more obvious than when he maligns his Creator. The "mystery of iniquity" will run its due course. Man scoffed at God's impending judgment during the days of Noah; man blasphemed God as Paul preached the gospel message (Acts 26:11), and, as previously stated, blasphemy of God will be unchecked during the future Tribulation Period. Thus, the increase of mankind's blasphemy against God is a sign of the end of the Church Age (2 Tim. 3:1-2).

## The Christian Response to Blasphemy

Believers should not take part in the desecration of God's name – Holy is His name! For many Christians, a relearning of righteous speech patterns and proper conduct to honor God's name are required. That the unsaved will lack reverence for the Lord's name is somewhat understandable, but why do Christians debase God's name in speech or in conduct, often unconscious of doing so? You may be thinking to yourself, "I don't blaspheme the Lord or show disrespect to His name!" However, this reflects a human understanding of what blasphemy is, not a biblical one. In actuality, in one form or another, we often unconsciously demean God's name. For example, how often have you heard someone say, "Holy ------"? This is a form of blasphemy, that is, taking what is high and holy and associating it with something earthly (it does not matter what it is), although it is often something putrid.

The problem of believers unconsciously debasing God's name seems to have been present even in the early church, for Paul exhorts believers more than once to put away all evil

## The Evil Nexus

speech and blasphemies (Eph. 4:31, Col. 3:8). Because Hymenaeus and Alexander had abandoned a good conscience and shipwrecked their faith, Paul committed them to the Lord in prayer, and unto Satan for buffeting. The end goal was *"that they may learn not to blaspheme"* (1 Tim. 1:20). William MacDonald comments on this passage:

> In the New Testament, *blaspheme* does not always mean to speak evil of God.... It might be used to describe the lives of these men as well as the words of their lips. By making shipwreck of the faith, they had undoubtedly caused others to speak evil of the way of truth, and thus their lives were living blasphemies.[4]

The Bible contains examples of individuals who blasphemed God and reveals that this sin will continue through the Church Age and into the Tribulation Period. God's exhortation to all believers is *"Be holy, for I am holy"* (1 Pet. 1:16). Not only are Christians not to speak blasphemy, but they must strive not to live blasphemy either (Jas. 2:7). God's will for the believer is that he or she should refrain from doing sin, and that he or she indeed practice a sin-free life altogether (1 Jn. 2:1). However, on this side of glory, sinless perfection is a pursuit, not a reality – thank God our salvation is not based on our doings, but upon His grace. And, praise be to God, our new nature received at conversion cannot sin (1 Jn. 3:9). Let us all pursue holiness, for in holiness we find not the inability to sin, but the ability not to sin.

Are you a blasphemer? Unfortunately, the answer is "yes," in the sense that we all are guilty of tarnishing the name of the Lord in one way or another – thus in this way Christians often unknowingly honor the devil. Either in word or deed, we have all communicated disdain for God's name and caused others to do the same. The more mindful we are of honoring God's name, the less likely we will be to possess carefree attitudes which predictably lead to offending God. Paul exhorted the believers

# #5 Blasphemy

at Colossae not to walk as they once did: *"But now you yourselves are to put off all these: anger, wrath, malice, blasphemy, filthy language out of your mouth"* (Col. 3:8). It is natural for an unsaved sinner to blaspheme God, for his or her fallen nature is at enmity with God – nothing in it can please God (Rom. 7:18).

However, a true believer has received a new nature and a new life (Gal. 2:20), and that nature seeks to exalt God, which requires putting to death continually the improper lusting of the flesh. In short, we are natural rebels against God, and regrettably, none of us walks as perfectly as he or she should. The reality of the matter is that we blaspheme the name of the Lord in a variety of ways. The tongue is the tail of the heart that wags out of the mouth – the depravity within our hearts, the rebellious nature within, eventually spews out of our mouths (Matt. 12:34-35).

It has already been shown that one can communicate blasphemy against the Lord through speech or other ungodly conduct. The following sins are some specific examples of the different forms of blasphemy noted in Scripture, that is, behavior which makes vain the name of the Lord and thus honors Satan.

**Teaching False Doctrine**

Teaching the Word of God to others is both a great privilege and a great responsibility that ultimately has accountability with God. Regarding this reality, James warned, *"My brethren, let not many of you become teachers, knowing that we shall receive a stricter judgment"* (Jas. 3:1). When a teacher opens the oracles of God to speak, he speaks for God. When an individual perverts the Word of God through traditions of men, vain philosophies, flawed music, or ignorance, he has misrepresented God and slandered God's name. Consider Paul's message to Timothy:

> *If anyone teaches otherwise and does not consent to wholesome words, even the words of our Lord Jesus Christ, and to the doctrine which accords with godliness, he is proud,*

## The Evil Nexus

*knowing nothing, but is obsessed with disputes and arguments over words, from which come envy, strife,* **reviling***, evil suspicions* (1 Tim. 6:3-4).

"Reviling" or "railings" (KJV) in the passage is translated from the same Greek word normally rendered "blasphemy." An individual who teaches, speaks, or sings false doctrine commits blasphemy against God because he or she perverts truth, thus causing God's holiness and perfection to be diminished and/or distorted in the minds of those listening.

**Swearing Falsely**

To swear is to strongly affirm a promise or statement by using the Lord's name. The activity of swearing to validate a promise was quite common in the Old Testament. The normal Hebrew word for swearing, *shaba*, which means "to swear'" or "to take an oath," is found 180 times in the Old Testament.

In the New Testament, however, the Lord Jesus traversed the high moral ground on the subject of swearing. He instructed His disciples, *"But let your communication be, Yea, yea; Nay, nay: for whatsoever is more than these cometh of evil"* (Matt. 5:37). The disciple of Christ does not need to swear to validate his or her words; the merit of everything said should be wholesome, accurate, needful, and gracious without adding God's name to it. Hence, the Lord issued a stern warning, *"But I say unto you,* **that every idle word** *that men shall speak, they shall give account thereof in the day of judgment. For by thy words thou shalt be justified, and by thy words thou shalt be condemned"* (Matt. 12:36-37). Lord, please forgive us for all our idle chit-chat and for allowing our tongues to flap in the wind!

Swearing involves tying God's name to our statements in an attempt to better validate what we say – to heighten the credibility of our words. The believer should not engage in such practices, for to do so would certainly bring low the name of God. Listen to James' warning for this sin, *"But above all things, my brethren, swear not, neither by heaven, neither by the earth,*

## #5 Blasphemy

*neither by any other oath: but let your yea be yea; and your nay, nay; lest ye fall into condemnation"* (Jas. 5:12). Demeaning the name of the Lord by swearing falsely is a terrible thing. As we are forgetful creatures and are rarely perfect in our speech, it behooves us to refrain from swearing oaths which we will most assuredly fall short of keeping. Certainly, the rash vows of Jephthah (Judg. 11:29-40) and Herod (Acts 12:20-23) serve as historical examples of the heavy price to be paid when one foolishly swears to God to do something.

An individual may be put into a position, such as in a court of law, where they would be placed under oath. These situations are rare, but sometimes are unavoidable. Perjury is a form of blasphemy, so if you are put "under oath," be diligent not to defame the Lord's name. *"And you shall not swear by My name falsely, nor shall you profane the name of your God: I am the Lord"* (Lev. 19:12) Swearing falsely has its consequences, for God does not forget:

> *"I will send out the curse,"* says the Lord of hosts; *"it shall enter the house of the thief and the house of the one who swears falsely by My name"* (Zech. 5:4).

The believer should always do his or her best to convey meaningful and accurate speech and to refrain from idle talk. *"Let no corrupt word proceed out of your mouth, but what is good for necessary edification, that it may impart grace to the hearers"* (Eph. 4:29). Solomon wisely concluded regarding the operation of our speech, *"Do not be rash with your mouth, and let not your heart utter anything hastily before God. For God is in heaven, and you on earth; therefore let your words be few"* (Eccl. 5:2). May all our profane speech be replaced with praise!

**Stealing**

*"Lest I be full and deny You, and say, 'Who is the Lord?' Or lest I be poor and steal, and profane the name of my God"* (Prov. 30:9). The writer requested that he neither be rich

## The Evil Nexus

(fearing he might forget the Lord) nor poor such that he might be forced to steal and, in so doing, disdain God's name. For this cause Paul exhorts believers to pursue the same Christ-honoring behavior: *"Let him who stole steal no longer, but rather let him labor, working with his hands what is good, that he may have something to give him who has need"* (Eph. 4:28). The Law was kept when one refrained from stealing, but the fulfilling of the law was accomplished through giving, not by not stealing (Rom. 13:8).

Proverbs illustrates that individuals can communicate blasphemy for the Lord's name without using actual words. We often say to our children, "actions speak louder than words," but we probably don't reckon the same truth in our breaking of God's laws. The believer sins because he or she chooses to, and our rebellious behavior insults God, affronts His holy character, and blasphemes His name. We cannot claim to be a Christian (a Christ-one) while we are diminishing His name through un-Christ-like conduct. Often, we think more about the personal consequences of our sin than we do about the hurt inflicted on the heart of God. Stealing offends God and degrades His name in the eyes of the unsaved.

**Demoting the Character of God**

One would have to wonder if anything pleases Satan more than when men curse and blaspheme the Lord. Peter engaged in intense cursing and repeated denial of the Lord while Christ was on trial; he found out just how weak his carnal weapons were against his flesh and the wiles of the devil. His cowardice and thoughts of self-preservation undermined the name of Christ (Matt. 26:74).

In the case of Job, twice Satan told God that *"he [Job] will surely curse You to Your face"* (Job 1:11; 2:5) if he were allowed to assault Job. Unfortunately, this very idea was given to Job by his wife, *"curse God and die"* (Job 2:9). Satan thoroughly enjoys dishonoring God and His name. Often overwhelming circumstances will cause a child of God to lose hope

## #5 Blasphemy

and lapse in his or her faith – strong faith is required to trust the hand which originated the billows and waves of adversity that crash upon our heads. Please note that God began the conversation with Satan concerning His servant Job. In other words, God nominated Job! The next nominee could be you or me.

Although Job did not curse God, he did sin against the Lord during his distress. The matter angered Bildad, and he reproved Job during their first dialogue (Job 8:1-7). What was the sin? Bildad accused Job of blaspheming God – speaking ill of God by questioning and accusing God of "wrongdoing." Though Bildad was a miserable counselor and consoler to Job, on this point the basis for his rebuke was correct, though not warranted, for God would personally address the matter with His servant Job later (Job 38).

Bildad's error was in informing Job that all his difficulties were a result of personal sin against God: *"Behold, God will not cast away the blameless, nor will He uphold the evildoers"* (Job 8:20, also 8:6). However, this was not the circumstance at all; Job's trial was not the chastening judgment of God resulting from Job's personal sin. God was obtaining glory out of Job's situation, while at the same time, further refining His servant who Scripture declares *"was blameless and upright, and one that feared God, and shunned evil"* (Job 1:1). On two separate occasions, God met with Job in a whirlwind to address his wrong attitudes – Job witnessed the holy and awesome nature of God firsthand. God's very character defines what is right; thus, He can do only what is pure, right and holy. God's very character is perfect moral light and whatever is in darkness is not of God – the lack of God's righteousness is the definition of evil (Isa. 45:5-7). The holiness of God enabled Job to better understand that God is righteous in all His ways.

During arduous circumstances, it is all too easy for the downcast and disheartened soul to think and say evil of God's doings. The fact is that God loves us too much to permit us to remain the way we are – He greatly desires for believers to reflect the moral glory of His Son to a world that desperately

# The Evil Nexus

needs to see Christ. Aggressive chiseling, chipping, sanding, and polishing are required to transform a chunk of granite into an attractive sculpture – and often God labors with hearts harder than granite. Our God is a God of promises, and we must simply trust Him in such arduous times and not question His character – He does have a plan, and it is marvelous (1 Cor. 10:13; Rom. 8:28).

If there were no God, our present sufferings would be overwhelming, for we would be a people without hope. But knowing that God is in all our woes and that He is personally working each out for our good and His glory affords joy in tribulations! In trials, let us maintain the up-look and not be guilty of looking down on God.

**The Impudent Heart**

In His pungent "Woe" message to the Pharisees, the Lord Jesus addressed the hypocritical act of swearing in a way which degraded the name of the Lord (Matt. 23:16-22). Although under a different guise, the same behavior is often witnessed today.

In esteeming the gold band that adorned the pinnacle of the temple more than the temple itself, the Pharisees were demonstrating disdain for God. Where is the value? In the gold or the temple? In the offering or the altar? The Lord bluntly told them that the altar gave value to the sacrifice, and that the temple bestowed the honor to the gold. The altar and the temple were patterned after holy heavenly realities (Heb. 9:23); each was directly connected to God. In placing the value on the offering and the gold, the Pharisees had disassociated themselves from God, but the Lord was telling them that only that which is connected with God has value; their traditions and swearing were just human nonsense and an insult to God.

The highest honor for gold would have been to be used in the house of God. The highest honor of a lamb in Judea was to be used as a sacrifice on the bronze altar. If gold and sheep had ambition, this would have been their highest calling. Christ was

## #5 Blasphemy

teaching that man apart from his connection with God is nothing; ambition apart from God is nothing; abilities apart from God are nothing! The only reason a believer can be honored before God is because of his or her association with Jesus Christ. Spurgeon once said to a believer, "The greatest thing about you is your connection with Calvary [Christ]."

The Lord Jesus wants our motives, our abilities and our entire life to be connected with Him. It is possible for us to ignorantly commit the same form of blasphemy that the Pharisees did (i.e. undervaluing our association with Christ). For example, the reader might have a brilliant mind. Some might say, "The Lord would be fortunate to have a mind like yours in His service." Wrong! That which is in association with Christ is what has the value. The right thinking is: "My greatest privilege in life is to use my talents for the Lord." Your intellect does not sanctify Jesus Christ, but Jesus Christ sanctifies your mind for His purpose and glory. Only those abilities that are submitted to the Lord can be used to honor Him and to bless the body of Christ.

Some time ago I heard William MacDonald tell the following story; I share it with you to illustrate the application of the Lord's message to the Pharisees:

> A number of years ago, while touring Paris, an American found an amber necklace in a secondhand street shop. It was marked with a low price, so he bought it. However, the customs officials really socked it to him with a duty tax when he reentered the US, which aroused his suspicion. He went to a jeweler who estimated its worth to be $25,000. He went to a second gemologist who said the necklace was worth $30,000. The man, being astounded, asked why it was worth so much. The jeweler handed him the magnifying glass and told him where to look on the necklace, where he read the inscription: "To Josephine from Napoleon." The necklace was not worth $30,000 in itself, but its association with Josephine and Napoleon made it valuable.

# The Evil Nexus

The same is true of you, dear believer. You only have value because of your association with Christ. We should not mock His Lordship and defame His name by thinking we have some ability or talent that He would do well to value and use. Such thinking is nothing less than hypocrisy and a pharisaical expression of pride – a form of blasphemy! Our highest service to the Lord is to be a living sacrifice, an emptied vessel of honor (2 Tim. 2:21) fitted for His sovereign use. If we live a holy, consecrated life, He will honor Himself; we need not presuppose our profitability to God.

In what ways might Christians be committing the same distorted thinking? Christian terminology or music which devalues the person and work of Christ or our association with Christ should be corrected. Continuously saying or singing something which is wrong, even if the matter seems trivial to us, in time becomes perceived truth in our thinking. The distinction between reality and fantasy becomes blurred when awareness to Scriptural truth is supplanted with indiscriminate familiarities, such as "The Lord is my buddy," or "The Man upstairs."

If the unsaved masses are to be reached for Christ in this present day, the Church must rethink its careless attitudes regarding how it represents and proclaims the name of Christ. Deliberate disregard for the Word of God, complacency over sin, and loss of reverence for the Lord's name have degraded the name of Christ throughout the world. The Church desperately needs revival! May we all repent and again esteem Christ above all things, *"that in all things He may have the preeminence"* (Col. 1:18), and may we fervently pray as Solomon did so long ago: *"That all peoples of the earth may know Your name and fear You, as do Your people"* (2 Chron. 6:33).

## Meditation

In the early morning of December 28, 1908, an earthquake totally destroyed the flourishing and extraordinarily beautiful city of Messina, Italy, and 75,000 human beings died. We

## #5 Blasphemy

read: "Only a few hours before that devastating earthquake, which laid Messina and the surrounding districts in ruins, the unspeakably wicked and irreligious condition of some of the inhabitants was expressed in a series of violent resolutions, which were passed against all religious principles. And the journal *Il Tleefono*, printed in Messina, actually published in its Christmas number an abominable parody daring the Almighty to make Himself known by sending an earthquake! And in three days He did!"[5]

# #6 Lying and Deception

Deception is akin to "lying," and both are evil tools of the devil. He deceives (i.e., blinds) the lost from understanding the gospel message that they might be saved (2 Cor. 4:4) and he beguiles believers into trading recognized truth for various humanized ideologies (2 Cor. 11:3). At the midpoint of the Tribulation Period, Satan will be cast out of heaven and constrained to the earth. Through a vision John witnesses this future event and describes what he saw: *"So the great dragon was cast out, that serpent of old, called the Devil and Satan, who deceives the whole world; he was cast to the earth, and his angels were cast out with him"* (Rev. 12:9). Later, John describes Satan's end and of those who were deceived into following him: *"The devil, who deceived them, was cast into the lake of fire and brimstone where the beast and the false prophet are. And they will be tormented day and night forever and ever"* (Rev. 20:10). Lies and deception are natural to the devil, and all of humanity has suffered loss because of these evil behaviors.

Lying is the willful stating of a falsehood, while deception is an attempt to cheat, delude, or seduce another's perception of the truth. Lying is a direct assault on the truth, while deception is a spin of the truth to cause a disoriented perception of it, usually for personal gain.

> A lie consists in speaking a falsehood with the intention of deceiving.
> — Augustine

Those engaging in lying and deception honor the devil and not the Lord Jesus. In confronting the pharisaical spirit of His

## The Evil Nexus

day, the Lord chided the Jewish religious leaders with the following rebuke:

> *You are of your father the devil, and the desires of your father you want to do. He was a murderer from the beginning, and does not stand in the truth, because there is no truth in him. When he speaks a lie, he speaks from his own resources, for he is a liar and the father of it* (John 8:44).

The devil is the "father of lies" – it is his nature to speak falsehoods and for those who follow him to do the same. If we always tell the truth, then we do not have to worry about what we said earlier. This is not the case with lying, for no man has a good enough memory to be a prosperous liar. Truth is eternal, but lies are short-lived. Solomon puts the matter this way, *"a lying tongue is but for a moment"* (Prov. 12:19). Most lies have a short lifespan, but certainly by the Great White Throne judgment of the wicked all deception and lies will be shown for what they are (Rev. 20:11-15).

> A little lie is like a little pregnancy – it doesn't take long before everyone knows.
> — C. S. Lewis

There are several biblical examples of God's people resorting to lying and deception when they felt there was no other alternative to escape the dire situation they were in. Scripture endorses Rahab's faith in her exploits to protect the two Jewish spies as recorded in Joshua 2, but not her lying to civil officials to do so. Rahab feared Jehovah and His people more than the king of Jericho and her fellow citizens (Josh. 2:11). She hence sided with Jehovah and the Hebrews, rather than those set to war against them. In her estimation deceiving the officials in order to prevent the capture of the two spies was an acceptable solution to her dilemma. However, God was perfectly able to protect them without Rahab's falsehoods to mislead the spies' pursuers. Despite the lie, the Lord responded to her faith and

## #6 Lying and Deception

rewarded her by sparing her life and the lives of those in her family who would also exercise faith in Jehovah (Josh. 6:25).

The midwives rejected Pharaoh's command to slaughter newborn Jewish boys because they feared God more than they did Pharaoh (Ex. 1:17). Therefore, the Hebrew midwives did not kill the baby boys as they were born. They then lied to Pharaoh in order to protect themselves from harm when he called them into question. Though they lied, God honored their faith: *"God dealt well with the midwives ... and He gave them families"* (Ex. 1:20-21). The Lord did not approve of their lying, for God is holy and He cannot wink at sin, no matter how justifiable it may seem through human reasoning.

Scripture repeatedly shows that God is able to work His will despite human falsehoods. Jacob lied and deceived Isaac, his father, in appropriating his brother Esau's birthright, but Jehovah had already stated it would be Jacob's inheritance. Widowed and mistreated Tamar lied to her father-in-law Judah in order to have children. As a fugitive among the Philistines, David acted insane before Achish to escape death. Hushai was David's spy in defiant Absalom's court; Absalom received him as a counselor because Absalom believed his lies, then Hushai defeated the counsel of Ahithophel and saved King David's life.

These examples are unique circumstances that all flow within the mainstream of messianic current – God's sovereign plan cannot be thwarted by the evil of the enemy, or by the sins of His people. Perhaps this understanding will help resolve any disparity in the reader's mind as to how a righteous God could bless His people despite their lying and deception. Is God capable of accomplishing His purposes without human deception and failure? Absolutely! Paul adamantly affirms this point: *"For what if some did not believe? Will their unbelief make the faithfulness of God without effect? Certainly not! Indeed, let God be true but every man a liar"* (Rom. 3:4). So let us, as God commands, be truth tellers, or if necessary to preserve justice and righteousness, let us say nothing at all and suffer the consequences with patience.

# The Evil Nexus

## Summary

God does not condone lying; He is able to work His will without the aid of human deception, and He is also able to maneuver the moral failures of man within His predetermined purposes. Yet sin, no matter how minor in our own eyes, has divine consequences for us. We should never justify telling falsehoods or deceiving others with a "the end justifies the means" mentality. Distortion of the truth does not honor God, and in fact, it demonstrates a lack of complete faith in His Word and sovereign control over creation.

> For not only does sound reason direct us to refuse the guidance of those who do or teach anything wrong, but it is by all means vital for the lover of truth, regardless of the threat of death, to choose to do and say what is right even before saving his own life.
> — A. W. Tozer

## The Christian Response to Lying and Deception

God is perfect; there are no degrees of holiness and righteousness in His character. Likewise, there are no shades to divine truth either; it is man and fallen spiritual beings who color, flavor, change, or dilute truth in direct opposition to God's authority. Consequently, Scripture forbids believers from engaging in lying or deception. There is no provision for lying; rather Paul exhorts, *"Putting away lying, let each one of you speak truth with his neighbor"* (Eph. 4:25) and *"speaking the truth in love, may grow up in all things into Him who is the head – Christ"* (Eph. 4:15). The Lord Jesus gave no endorsement of deception either: *"But let your 'Yes' be 'Yes,' and your 'No,' 'No.' For whatever is more than these is from the evil one"* (Matt 5:37). In fact, believers are not only to refrain from being deceptive when interacting with others, they are to labor to not be deceived also.

Paul admonished the believers at Ephesus not to be like *"children, tossed to and fro and carried about with every wind*

## #6 Lying and Deception

*of doctrine, by the trickery of men, in the cunning craftiness of deceitful plotting"* (Eph. 4:14). False teachers, propagating satanic doctrines, were rampant in Paul's day and perhaps even more so in these last days of the Church Age. Let us continuously review Scripture and evaluate our conduct, terminology, and language, lest in time, unbiblical expressions and traditions develop, causing us to err from the truth. John tells us that every believer has a spiritual anointing of the Holy Spirit to provide discernment in matters of divine truth (1 Jn. 2:18-27).

During Old Testament times, priests, prophets, and kings were often anointed with oil when consecrated to serve the Lord. The Lord Jesus Himself was anointed by the Holy Spirit at the commencement of His ministry (Matt. 3:16; Acts 10:38). Likewise, each believer is anointed and called to serve the body of Christ according to God's will (Eph. 2:10). Not only does this anointing separate out the believer for God's purpose, but the anointing actually provides spiritual discernment of the truth, which enables the believer to follow after God's will in his or her ministry. This spiritual anointing occurs once at conversion, it is never repeated, and it is always referred to in the past tense (2 Cor. 1:21; 1 Jn. 2:20). This anointing provides discernment between truth and deception (1 Jn. 2:27), and should not be prayed for, as is often the case – the believer already has the only anointing they will ever receive.

This anointing enables the believer to understand God's Word and to have an accurate sense of what it means. While it is true that some godly, seasoned believers may disagree on the outworking of doctrine, the essentials of Scriptural truth should be held in unity, that is, if each believer is honestly seeking the truth and is being led by the Holy Spirit. This does not mean that Scripture is easy to understand; in fact, the opposite is true. The natural man, apart from God's help, cannot understand the things of God (1 Cor. 2:10-12). Thus, time and energy must be expended in Scripture to lay hold of the truth accurately: *"Be diligent to present yourself approved to God, a worker who does not need to be ashamed, rightly dividing the word of truth"*

# The Evil Nexus

(2 Tim. 2:15). Knowing what Scripture means is the believer's main line of defense against being deceived by fanciful speech and intellectual arguments.

The best way in the world to deceive believers is to cloak a message in religious language and declare that it conveys some new insight from God.
— Charles Stanley

Paul exhorted the Christians at Philippi to *"prove* [or distinguish] *the things that differ"* (Phil. 1:10, R.V.). Wuest's expanded translation puts it this way: "recognize the true value of finer distinctions involved in Christian conduct and then sanctify them."[1] The doctrines of men often develop from carelessly dividing God's Word, or through the complacency of not correcting what is known to be not quite right. Often these matters are only slight distortions in truth and really don't arouse much attention until after the harm is realized long afterwards: *"Buy the truth, and do not sell it"* (Prov. 23:23).

## Meditation

Satan rarely presents outright lies; rather, he depends upon a series of blurred deceptions to gain His footing and to wreak havoc within the Church. I will illustrate this point: "Despite what you might have thought previously, *black* really means *white*." You say, "No, black is the opposite of white." But then I pick up a reliable dictionary, say *The American Heritage Dictionary*[2], and show you that the meaning of "black" is "dark," and then I confirm that one of the meanings of "dark" is "dim." Finding the entry for "dim" I prove to you that "dim" can denote "pale." And finally I look up the word "pale" and verify that one of the connotations of "pale" is "white." I have proven to you using a series of only four imprecise meanings (variations of the best meaning, if you will) that *black* is equal to *white*. If the devil can deceive the believer into compromising even a small portion of the truth, be sure that he will return to

## #6 Lying and Deception

accomplish the same objective again and again. He may wait a bit until we become comfortable in our complacency, but He will always come back! Standing fast in the truth and resisting his attempts is our security against being lured into compromise and engaging in the sins of lying and deception (1 Pet. 5:8-9).

# #7 Gossip

The sins of gossip and slander are closely related as shown by Proverbs 20:19 (NAS): *"He who goes about as a slanderer reveals secrets, therefore do not associate with a gossip."* Paul listed these sins side by side when he exhorted the believers at Corinth to repute ungodly conduct: *"For I am afraid that perhaps when I come I may find you to be not what I wish and may be found by you to be not what you wish; that perhaps there may be strife, jealousy, angry tempers, disputes, slanders, gossip, arrogance, disturbances"* (2 Cor. 12:20; NAS). The two Greek words translated "slanders" and "gossip" in this verse are more vividly rendered "backbitings" and "whisperings" in the KJV and NKJV translations of the Bible.

The first Greek word *katalalia* means "to defame one's character," while the second word *psithurismos* refers to "secretly uttering an untruth or attempt to deceive by falsehood." Apparently, some people will believe anything if it is whispered in their ear. Accordingly, gossip rarely propagates the truth, nor does it have the good of others as an objective; rather, it is a device of the devil to cast doubt on the integrity of another person and damage them in the eyes of others.

Gossip has been widely described as the art of saying nothing in a way that leaves nothing unsaid. Often it is jealousy, envy, or unresolved anger that prompts people to gossip about others. Someone with a bitter and resentful heart, for example, will be prone to jab, gossip, dig, avoid, imagine evil and adopt guerrilla warfare tactics to achieve discrete revenge. In the end, their festering anger will adversely affect all relationships with others, including their fellowship with God. Whether by bitterness, jealousy, or envy, these self-imposed emotional states first afflict us, and then we harm others through devilish behaviors

## The Evil Nexus

such as gossip and slander. These internalized ill feelings are like voluntarily drinking poison and waiting for the other person to die or locking yourself in a caliginous dungeon and then feeling superior while you slowly watch yourself rot away.

> Tale-bearing emits a threefold poison, for it injures the teller, the hearer and the person concerning whom the tale is told.
>
> — Charles Spurgeon

Emphatically stated, gossip, which is a milder and more covert form of slander, is sin! Sometimes gossip manifests itself in the strangest formats, such as prayer requests, compliments, and as a "just for your information" bulletin. If you are not part of the problem or the solution in a particular matter, it is usually best not to get involved; just be quiet and do not bend your ear to evil whisperings. It is our nature to jump to conclusions without all the facts and then deliberately and ungraciously share these presumptuous judgments with others. Such behavior, at best, distorts the truth concerning the guilty and at its worst defames and defrauds the innocent. God is not honored in either case.

*In the multitude of words sin is not lacking. But he who restrains his lips is wise* (Prov. 10:19).

*There is one who speaks like the piercings of a sword, but the tongue of the wise promotes health* (Prov. 12:18).

*A prudent man conceals knowledge, but the heart of fools proclaims foolishness* (Prov. 12:23).

*He who covers a transgression seeks love, but he who repeats a matter separates friends* (Prov. 17:9).

U. S. Naval Admiral Hyman Rickover summarized gossip this way, "Great minds discuss ideas. Average minds discuss

## #7 Gossip

events. Small minds discuss people."[1] The spiritual mind muses upon Christ and eternal truth. So dear reader, what kind of mind do you have? The tongue is the tail of the heart that wags out of the mouth, for *"those things which proceed out of the mouth come from the heart, and they defile a man"* (Matt. 15:18). Whatever is in your heart will eventually come out your mouth.

### Summary

Gossip is like a dangerous virus that sweeps through whole communities through personal interaction. It secretly infects each person it comes in contact with, unless that person has acquired immunity against it. The consequences of this dangerous infection are realized much later, and may be long lasting, even resulting in death. Gossip, or slanderous whispering, does not propagate the truth in love, but has the objective of degrading another's character, thus damaging his or her reputation and ministry. Those who repeat gossip needlessly infect others with this dangerous virus. Praise God for those who are immune to this sin as shown by not listening to, or repeating, what would needlessly infect others with evil and inevitably cause them harm.

> I will speak ill of no man, not even in the matter of truth, but rather excuse the faults I hear, and, upon proper occasions, speak all the good I know of everybody.
>
> — Benjamin Franklin

### The Christian Response to Gossip

Believers are not to be contentious people; we should not be prone to gossip or slander, knowing that unjust and unneeded talk can do irreparable damage to one's good name and testimony. What is said about others should be true (based on the facts), stated gently (in the spirit of genuine love and concern), and only done if necessary to prevent others from being hurt and for the edification of the subject party.

# The Evil Nexus

Solomon likens the sin of propagating gossip to throwing more wood on a fire:

*Where there is no wood, the fire goes out; and where there is no talebearer, strife ceases. As charcoal is to burning coals, and wood to fire, so is a contentious man to kindle strife* (Prov. 26:20-21).

Physical law has determined that there are basically two ways to stop a chemical reaction which produces a flame: by removing either the fuel or the oxygen from the combustion process. Solomon uses this similitude to teach us how to stop gossip. First, do not allow the gossiper to whisper in your ear; that stops the gossip from spreading as you did not become aware of the information. This response removes wood from the fire, so to speak: If the gossip is not heard and repeated, the rumor soon dies out. Second, pouring water on a fire robs the combustion reaction of needed air, which abruptly extinguishes the flame. This resembles the proactive behavior of bringing the gossip and gossiper to the attention of the one being hurt by it. When this happens, the truth of the matter quickly comes out and the gossip is dealt a deadly blow and the gossiper is rebuked by his or her own folly.

One Sunday morning a well-intentioned individual pulled me aside during a break between church meetings. This individual began to gossip about another Christian. I raised my hand to stop the gossiper's dialogue and said, "Just a moment. This brother is just in the next room; I will retrieve him and be right back." Not only did this impromptu meeting between the three of us correct the rumor and stop the gossip, but it also prevented future gossip coming to me from the now sorrowful gossiper. Knowing how I would handle the situation in the future ensured that this individual would not be gossiping to me thereafter. Dear believer, when gossip comes your way, and it will, yank the wood and throw the water! To do so shows love and care for other believers and the realization that the ministry they

## #7 Gossip

are engaged in is truly important to you. Protect the work of the Lord; too much is at stake to allow this destructive behavior to go unchecked. Let us pray for and encourage each other with our tongues, rather than using them to destroy what Jesus Christ is laboring diligently to build.

> Notice, we never pray for folks we gossip about, and we never gossip about the folks for whom we pray! For prayer is a great deterrent.
> — Leonard Ravenhill

This type of mutual love and respect for others was demonstrated by a group of men, including John Wesley, who were nicknamed Methodists. In 1752, they all signed a covenant which every man might hang on his study wall. The six articles of the solemn agreement follow:

1. That we will not listen or willingly inquire after ill concerning one another;
2. That, if we do hear any ill of each other, we will not be forward to believe it;
3. That as soon as possible we will communicate what we hear by speaking or writing to the person concerned;
4. That until we have done this, we will not write or speak a syllable of it to any other person;
5. That neither will we mention it, after we have done this, to any other person;
6. That we will not make any exception to any of these rules unless we think ourselves absolutely obliged in conference.[2]

May we be a truth telling, love motivated, and necessity speaking people. So much damage has been done to those that the Lord Jesus bled and died for through slanderous whisperings. We may have a righteous reason to be offended and be angry with another believer, but let us not behave like children of disobedience at such times. Rather, let us speak the truth in

## The Evil Nexus

love and muster up the courage to address the matter expediently and privately with the offender, so that we limit the devil's reach into our hearts and through our lips. We do well to remember that whoever gossips to you will gossip of you. Adopt the adage – "Don't listen, and if you do, don't tell."

## Meditation

The following is a true story illustrates the destructive and sad consequences of gossip:

> They were a happy little family, living in a small town in North Dakota, even though the young mother had not been entirely well since the birth of her second baby. But each evening the neighbors were aware of a warmth in their hearts when they would see the husband and father being met at the gate by his wife and two small children. There was laughter in the evening too, and when the weather was nice Father and children would romp together on the back lawn while Mother looked on with happy smiles.
>
> Then one day a village gossip started a story, saying that he was being unfaithful to his wife, a story entirely without foundation. But it eventually came to the ears of the young wife, and it was more than she could bear. Reason left its throne, and that night when her husband came home, there was no one to meet him at the gate, no laughter in the house, no fragrant aroma coming from the kitchen—only coldness and something that chilled his heart with fear.
>
> And down in the basement he found the three of them hanging from a beam. Sick and in despair, the young mother had first taken the lives of her two children, and then her own. In the days that followed, the truth of what had happened came out – a gossip's tongue, an untrue story, a terrible tragedy.[3]

# The Real Enemy of the Real Battle

Paul reminded the believers at Ephesus that the real battle was not with flesh and blood, (i.e. people in the world), but rather *"against principalities, against powers, against the rulers of the darkness of this age, against spiritual hosts of wickedness in the heavenly places"* (Eph. 6:12-13). The ringleader of the powers of darkness is Satan. He consistently opposed the Lord Jesus Christ throughout His earthly ministry and today he continues to oppose the gospel message of Jesus Christ and those who would spread it. Satan despises Christ and those who identify with Him; accordingly, the devil works to manipulate various world systems of thinking to exclude Christ from consideration.

As previously stated, Satan is identified as *"the god of this age"* (2 Cor. 4:4), *"the prince of the power of the air"* (Eph. 2:2), and *"the prince of this world"* (John 12:31, 14:30, 16:11). The world is Satan's delegated domain, but he must function within divine boundaries. God is holy, and He cannot tempt anyone to sin (Jas. 1:13), although Satan is allowed to test man's resolve to obey God. In the days of Joshua, the Gibeonites, Satan's tricksters, were permitted to test God's people; unfortunately, they were deceived and in ignorance disobeyed the Lord. The consequences of not seeking the Lord's counsel in that one ingenious ruse were centuries of pain and suffering. The Gibeonites, so to speak, are still dwelling among us today and they continue to challenge our resolve to submit to God's Word through elaborate deception and clever reasoning.

Consequently, the real war will not be won with earthly resources or by our finest efforts, but only with heavenly power:

# The Evil Nexus

*Finally, my brethren, be strong in the Lord and in the power of His might. Put on the whole armor of God, that you may be able to stand against the wiles of the devil. For we do not wrestle against flesh and blood, but against principalities, against powers, against the rulers of the darkness of this age, against spiritual hosts of wickedness in the heavenly places. Therefore take up the whole armor of God, that you may be able to withstand in the evil day, and having done all, to stand* (Eph. 6:10-13).

*For though we walk in the flesh, we do not war according to the flesh. For the weapons of our warfare are not carnal but mighty in God for pulling down strongholds, casting down arguments and every high thing that exalts itself against the knowledge of God* (2 Cor. 10:3-5).

The real enemy is not the atheist who mocks our faith, but spiritual wickedness in heavenly places. The proper defense against such an enemy is not our money, fame, organizing, wit, or intellect, but spiritual armor. The effectual weapons of warfare are prayer and the sword of the Spirit (i.e., God's Word rightly applied and empowered by the Holy Spirit). So if the real war is against spiritual wickedness in high places, that is where we must engage the enemy. What are our resources there? *"Blessed be the God and Father of our Lord Jesus Christ, who has blessed us with every spiritual blessing in the heavenly places in Christ"* (Eph. 1:3). Beloved of the Lord, the real battle can only be won through utter dependency on the Lord. A solider of the cross must be energized through prayer, clad with spiritual armor, and able to wield the sword of truth with precision and divine enablement.

The devil's main ambition is to lead as many of those who were created in God's image away from Him and the salvation He offers. This realization is shown to us in Genesis 14 where the King of Sodom is used as allegorical depiction of Satan. The King of Sodom ruled over a wicked domain, he had been overthrown, and he did not care for the spoil reclaimed by Abraham,

# The Real Enemy of the Real Battle

but rather wanted only the souls that Abraham had rescued. As Satan knows his doom is sealed (Rev. 12:12, 20:10), he is determined to lead as many as possible into the eternal flames of hell (Rev. 13:15, 19:20-21). The interchange between the King of Sodom and Abraham reminds us that Satan's desire is to keep souls from turning to Christ that they might be saved (1 Tim. 5:15; 2 Thess. 2:9-10) and that he will let Christians have their "stuff" as a means to accomplish this objective.

The prophet Ezekiel informs us that before his fall, Lucifer was a beautiful cherub, sheathed with precious stones and inherently equipped with musical ability (Ezek. 28:11-16). He is likely the most powerful being that God created and, thus, is a cunning and dangerous enemy, one that only God can control. Accordingly, believers are not commanded to confront Satan directly, but rather to resist him by submitting to God in faith (Jas. 4:7). The devil will not waste his time on resisting believers, but will rather depart from them to find others who are not.

Believers are to be knowledgeable of his tactics so that he does not gain an advantage over them through ignorance (2 Cor. 2:11). Because Satan repeatedly uses the same strategies to oppose the things of God, believers are able to become more aware of his confrontational tactics by obtaining counsel from God's Word. His tactics include: forging unnatural unions between God's people and his, casting doubt on God's Word, undermining the person and work of Christ, soliciting us to lust for what is outside of God's will, stirring up strife and division among God's people, promoting self-awareness and self-serving attitudes, using deception and lies to hide the truth, and prompting religious pride wherever possible.

If believers truly understand the real enemy and the real battle, they will be careful not to do the devil's bidding by engaging in disobedience, false accusations, slander, strife causing divisions, blasphemy, deception, lying, and gossip – these are devilish tools used to war against and harm the Church of Jesus Christ. Rather, Paul affirms what the child of God's conduct should be: *"Whatever you do, do all to the glory of God. Give*

## The Evil Nexus

*no offense, either to the Jews or to the Greeks or to the Church of God"* (1 Cor. 10:31-32). Let those who have experienced spiritual rebirth no more behave like children of the devil, but rather, let them walk in the newness of life as children of light!

*Therefore be imitators of God as dear children. And walk in love, as Christ also has loved us and given Himself for us, an offering and a sacrifice to God for a sweet-smelling aroma. But fornication and all uncleanness or covetousness, let it not even be named among you, as is fitting for saints; neither filthiness, nor foolish talking, nor coarse jesting, which are not fitting, but rather giving of thanks. For this you know, that no fornicator, unclean person, nor covetous man, who is an idolater, has any inheritance in the kingdom of Christ and God. Let no one deceive you with empty words, for because of these things the wrath of God comes upon the sons of disobedience. Therefore do not be partakers with them. For you were once darkness, but now you are light in the Lord. Walk as children of light (for the fruit of the Spirit is in all goodness, righteousness, and truth), finding out what is acceptable to the Lord.* **And have no fellowship with the unfruitful works of darkness, but rather expose them** (Eph. 5:1-11).

Being imitators of God as His dear children ensures that we will not be in league with Satan against our dear Savior. By God's grace believers have been delivered from spiritual death and the bondage of sin; therefore, may we never collaborate with the enemy again. There is no biblical reason for a child of God to willfully, or ignorantly, aid the devil in his rebellion against our heavenly Father!

# Endnotes

## The Evil Nexus
1. https://www.barna.org/barna-update/article/12-faithspirituality/260-most-american-christians-do-not-believe-that-satan-or-the-holy-spirit-exis#.UrMXYeLYCSo
2. https://www.barna.org/barna-update/article/21-transformation/252-barna-survey-examines-changes-in-worldview-among-christians-over-the-past-13-years#.UrMceuLYCSo
3. P. L. Tan, *Encyclopedia of 7700 illustrations* (Bible Communications, Garland TX; 1996, c1979); devil

## The Ongoing Unseen Conflict
1. J. H. Thayer, *Thayer's Greek Lexicon* (Biblesoft; 2000), electronic database
2. S. Emery, *Treasury of Bible Doctrine – Mediator and Advocate* (Precious Seed Magazine, UK: 1977), p. 210
3. James Gunn, *Christ The Fullness of the Godhead* (Loizeaux Brothers, Neptune, NJ: 1982), p. 167
4. J. Vernon McGee, "Hosea Study Guide: Introduction," from *Thru the Bible Commentary, Vol. 27: Hosea & Joel* (Thomas Nelson Publishers, Nashville, TN, 1991)

## #1 Disobedience
1. F. W. Grant, *Genesis in the Light – The Serious Christian Series* (Loizeaux Brothers, Inc., Neptune, NJ), p. 39
2. Warren Henderson, *The Bible: Myth or Divine Truth?* (Warren A. Henderson, Pomona, KS; 2007), pp. 27-28
3. P. L. Tan, *Encyclopedia of 7700 illustrations* (Bible Communications, Garland TX; 1996, c1979); Bible Memorization

## #2 False Accusations
1. Francis Frangipane, *Exposing the Accuser of the Brethren* (Arrow Publications, Cedar Rapids, IA; 1994), excerpts
2. William MacDonald, *True Discipleship* (Gospel Folio Press, Port Colborne, ON; 2003), p. 155
3. P. L. Tan, *Encyclopedia of 7700 illustrations* (Bible Communications, Garland TX; 1996, c1979); Criticism

# The Evil Nexus

## #3 Slander
1. H. A. Ironside, *Notes on the Book of Ezra* (Shiloh Christian Library, no date); p. 71
2. P. L. Tan, op. cit., Gossip
3. http://christian-quotes.ochristian.com/christian-quotes_ochristian.cgi?query=slander&action=Search&x=0&y=0

## #4 Strife and Division
1. H. A. Ironside, *Proverbs* (Loizeaux Brothers, Neptune, NJ; 1995), p. 87
2. R. C. Chapman, *Robert Cleaver Chapman of Barnstaple*, by W. H. Bennet (Pickering & Inglis, Glasgow, Scotland; 1st ed.), pp. 125-126
3. William MacDonald, *Believer's Bible Commentary* (Thomas Nelson Pub., Nashville, TN; 1990), p. 1217

## #5 Blasphemy
1. Charles Hodge, *Systematic Theology* (Logos Research Systems, Inc., Oak Harbor, WA; 1997 – electronic copy)
2. Warren Wiersbe, *Be Holy: An Old Testament Study—Leviticus* (Victor Books, Wheaton, IL; 1994 – electronic copy)
3. Matthew Henry, *Matthew Henry's Commentary on the Whole Bible* (Hendrickson, Peabody, MA; 1991 – electronic version)
4. William MacDonald, *Believer's Bible Commentary* (Thomas Nelson Publishers, Nashville, TN; 1989), p. 2080
5. P. L. Tan, *Encyclopedia of 7700 illustrations* (Bible Communications, Garland TX; 1996, c1979); Blasphemer

## #6 Lying and Deception
1. Kenneth S. Wuest, *The New Testament: An Expanded Translation* (Eerdmans Publishing Co., Grand Rapids, MI; 1989), Phil. 1:10
2. *The American Heritage Dictionary* (Houghton Mifflin Company, Boston, MA; 1978)

## #7 Gossip
1. William MacDonald, *The Disciple's Manual* (Gospel Folio Press, Port Colborne, ON: 2004), p. 290
2. P. L. Tan, *Encyclopedia of 7700 illustrations* (Bible Communications, Garland TX; 1996, c1979); Gossip
3. Ibid.

# HALLOWED BE THY NAME

## Revering CHRIST in a casual World

Is scriptural terminology important? Does wrong terminology tend to lead to erroneous Church practices? Do I ignorantly show disdain for the Lord's name by the way in which I address Him or speak of Him to others? What is the sin of blasphemy? Can a Christian blaspheme God today? These are some of the questions *Hallowed Be Thy Name* examines in detail. Our speech and behaviour reflect our heart's adoration for the Lord Jesus and, thus, directly affect our testimony of Him to the world. May God bestow us grace to *"buy the truth, and sell it not"* (Prov. 23:23), and may each one be subject to the *"good, and acceptable, and perfect, will of God"* (Rom. 12:2).

**Binding:** Paper
**Size:** 5.5" X 8.5"
**Page Count:** 160 pages
**Item #:** B-7450
**ISBN:** 1-897117-45-0
**Genre:** Christian Living

### Warren Henderson

An aerospace engineer, who now serves the Lord with his wife Brenda in "full time" ministry. They are commended by Believers Bible Chapel in Rockford, Illinois. Warren is an itinerant Bible teacher and is involved in writing, evangelism, and church planting.

## GOSPEL FOLIO PRESS
I WILL PUBLISH THE NAME OF THE LORD

304 Killaly St. West | Port Colborne | ON | L3K 6A6 | Canada | 1 800 952 2382 | E-mail: info@gospelfolio.com | www.gospelfolio.com

# BEHOLD THE SAVIOUR

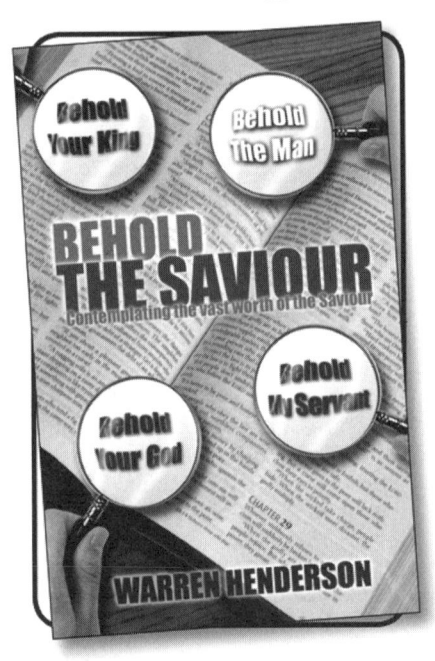

## CONTEMPLATING THE VAST WORTH OF THE SAVIOUR

It was refreshing and encouraging to read a book, that did not focus on man's needs or a "how to" method for success. *Behold the Saviour* focuses on the Lord Jesus: His Godhood, human goodness and glories as revealed in the multi-faceted presentation of Holy Scriptures. For when we behold Him in His glory we are *"changed into the same image from glory to glory, even as by the Spirit of the Lord"* (2 Cor. 3:18).

—Anonymous Pre-Publication Reviewer
(to Christ be the glory!)

Charles Haddon Spurgeon once said, "The more you know about Christ, the less you will be satisfied with superficial views of Him." The more we know of Christ, the more we will love and experience Him. This study has refreshed my soul. In the long hours of contemplating the vast worth that the Father attaches to every aspect of the Saviour's life, I have been encouraged to love Him more. If you're feeling a bit dry or spiritually despondent, *Behold the Saviour* afresh – and may the Holy Spirit ignite your passion for Christ and invigorate your ministry for Him. —Warren Henderson

**Binding:** Paper
**Size:** 5.5" X 8.5"
**Page Count:** 208 pages
**Item #:** B-7272
**ISBN :** 1-897117-27-2
**Genre:** Devotional

### Warren Henderson

An aerospace engineer, who now serves the Lord with his wife Brenda in "full time" ministry. They are commended by Believers Bible Chapel in Rockford, Illinois. Warren is an itinerant Bible teacher and is involved in writing, evangelism, and church planting.

## GOSPEL FOLIO PRESS
I WILL PUBLISH THE NAME OF THE LORD

304 Killaly St. West | Port Colborne | ON | L3K 6A6 | Canada | 1 800 952 2382 | E-mail: info@gospelfolio.com | www.gospelfolio.com

## Overcoming Your Bully

### Warren Henderson

*"The flesh"* describes the natural man. God has no program to change the flesh. Rather He brings in something new: *"and that which is born of the Spirit is spirit"* (John 3:6). A new struggle is brought to our attention. It is no longer the new nature or the believer striving for mastery over sin in the body; it is the Holy Spirit striving against the old nature. The little boy coming home from school was beaten up by a big bully. He was on the bottom, and the big bully was pounding him very heavily. Then he looked up from his defeated position on the bottom, and saw his big brother coming. The big brother took care of the bully while the little fellow crawled up on a stump and rubbed his bruises. The believer has the Holy Spirit to deal with the flesh, that big bully. I learned along time ago that I can't overcome it. So I have to turn it over to Somebody who can. The Holy Spirit indwells believers. He wants to do that for us, and He can!

—from the Preface by James Vernon McGee

A timely book, in a day when many believer's lives, marriages and ministries are being destroyed by being too easy on the flesh. Here is a call to give no quarter to the flesh but to be like Phinehas of old, and Ram the javelin home! Read it, meditate on it, and most of all apply it!    —Mike Attwood

ISBN: 9781926765358 ✦ US: $11.99 ✦ CDN: $12.99 ✦ Pages: 136

# Hiding God

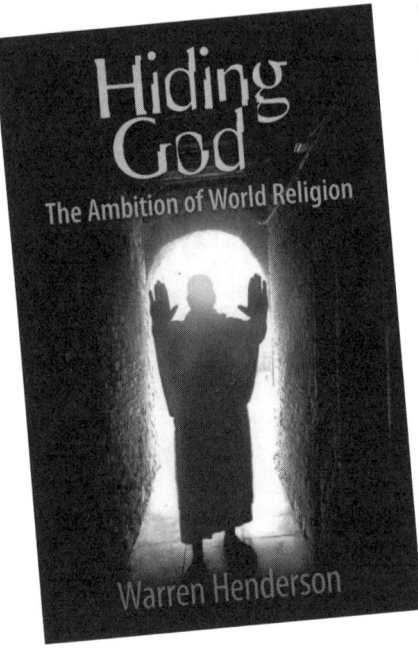

## The Ambition of World Religion

World religion is an exhaustive system of doings apart from God's truth and enablement. Ask yourself...

* How does world religion obscure divine truth and prevent man from knowing God?
* What general trends are consistently found in humanized religion?
* What advantage does biblical Christianity have over the religions of the world?
* Why should I trust Jesus Christ alone to secure eternal life?

Examine the evidence and determine for yourself if biblical Christianity is a logical choice.

### PB | X-8711 | Retail $9.99
(Shipping & Handling Extra)

**Warren Henderson** was an aerospace engineer, he now serves the Lord with his wife Brenda in "full time" ministry. They are commended by Believers Bible Chapel in Rockford, Illinois. Warren is an itinerant Bible teacher and is involved in writing, evangelism, and church planting. He is the author of *Be Angry and Sin Not, Behold The Saviour, The Fruitful Vine, The Olive Plants, Glories Seen and Unseen, Hallowed Be Thy Name, Mind Frames, Seeds of Destiny,* and *Your Home: A Birthing Place of Heaven.*

## GOSPEL FOLIO PRESS
To Order: Call 1-800-952-2382 | Email: orders@gospelfolio.com | www.gospelfolio.com